Yours
T. De Witt Talmage

I0754173

NIGHT SCENES

OF

CITY LIFE

BY

T. DEWITT TALMAGE, D. D.,

AUTHOR OF "CRUMBS SWEPT UP," "AROUND THE TEA TABLE,"
"SPORTS THAT KILL," "LIVE COALS,"
ETC., ETC.

CHICAGO:
DONOHUE, HENNEBERRY & CO.
1891.

PRINTED AND BOUND BY
DONOHUE & HENNEBERRY,
CHICAGO.

AUTHOR'S PREFACE.

The following discourses were stenographically reported, and by me revised for publication, expressly for the only authorized publishers.

T. DeWitt Talmage.

PUBLISHER'S PREFACE.

In issuing this collection from our press we do it in the profound conviction that the Christian community and the great American Public in general will appreciate these soul-stirring discourses on the temptations and vices of city life, by Dr. Talmage as seen by him in his midnight explorations in the haunts of vice of New York City, with his exposure of the traps and pitfalls that tempt our youth from the path of rectitude. They are written in his strongest descriptive powers, sparkling with graceful images and illustrative anecdotes; terrible in their earnestness; uncompromising in denunciation of sin and wickedness among the high or low, sparing neither rich nor poor; and are Dr. Talmage's best efforts in his earnest, aggressive warfare against the foes of society, every page burning with eloquent entreaty for a better, purer life, and are of intense, soul-absorbing interest to all who look for the advancement and higher development of the human race. This work is the ONLY REVISED AND AUTHORIZED publication of Dr. Talmage's sermons.

CONTENTS.

CHAPTER I.

A PERSONAL EXPLORATION IN HAUNTS OF VICE.

CHAPTER II.

LEPERS OF HIGH LIFE.

CHAPTER III.

THE GATES OF HELL.

CHAPTER IV.

WHOM I SAW AND WHOM I MISSED.

CHAPTER V.

UNDER THE POLICE LANTERN.

CHAPTER VI.

SATANIC AGITATION.

CHAPTER VII.

AMONG THIEVES AND ASSASSINS.

CHAPTER VIII.

CLUB-HOUSES—LEGITIMATE AND ILLEGITIMATE.

CHAPTER IX.

POISON IN THE CALDRON.

CHAPTER X.

THE CART ROPE INIQUITY.

CHAPTER XI.

THE WOMAN OF PLEASURE.

CHAPTER XII.

THE SINS OF SUMMER WATERING PLACES.

CHAPTER XIII.

THE TIDES OF MUNICIPAL SIN.

CHAPTER XIV.

RESPONSIBILITY OF CITY RULERS.

CHAPTER XV.

SAFEGUARDS FOR YOUNG MEN.

CHAPTER XVI.

THE VOICES OF THE STREET.

CHAPTER XVII.

HEROES IN COMMON LIFE.

CHAPTER XVIII.

THE MIDNIGHT HORSEMAN.

T. DE WITT TALMAGE, D. D.

Thomas DeWitt Talmage was born in 1832, in Bound Brook, Somerset County, N. J. His father was a farmer of much vigor and consistency of character; his mother a woman of noted energy, hopefulness and equanimity. Both parents were in marked respects characteristic. Differences of disposition and methods blended in them into a harmonious, consecrated, benignant and cheery life. The father won all the confidence and the best of the honors a hard-sensed truly American community had to yield. The mother was that counseling and quietly provident force which made her a helpmeet indeed and her home the center and sanctuary of the sweetest influences that have fallen on the path of a large number of children, of whom four sons are all ministers of the Word. From a period ante-dating the Revolution, the ancestors of our subject were members of the Reformed Dutch Church, in which Dr Talmage's father was the leading lay office bearer through a life extended beyond fourscore years. The youngest of the children, it seemed doubtful at first whether DeWitt would follow his brothers into the ministry. His earliest preference was the law, the studies of which he pursued for a year after his graduation with honors from the University of the City of New York. The faculties which would have made him the greatest jury advocate of the age were, however, preserved for and directed toward the pulpit by an unrest which took the very sound of a cry within him for months, "Woe is me if I preach not the gospel." When he submitted to it the always ardent but never urged hopes of his honored parents were realized. He entered the ministry from the New Brunswick Seminary of Theology. As his destiny and powers came to manifestation in Brooklyn, his pastoral life prior to that was but a preparation for it. It can, therefore, be indicated as an incidental stage in his career rather than treated at length as a principal part of it. His first settlement was at Belleville, on the beautiful Passaic, in New Jersey. For three years there he underwent an excellent practical education in the conventional ministry. His congregation was about the most cultivated and exacting in the rural regions of the sterling little state. Historically, it was known to be about the oldest society of Protestantism in New Jersey. Its records, as preserved, run back over 200 years, but it is known to have had a strong life the better part of a century more. Its structure is regarded as one of the finest of any country congregation in the United States. No wonder: it stands within rifle-shot of the quarry from which Old Trinity in New York was hewn. The value (and the limits) of stereotyped preaching and what he did *not* know came as an instructive and disillusionizing force to the theological tyro at Belleville. There also came and remained strong friendships, inspiring revivals, and sacred counsels.

By natural promotion three years at Syracuse succeeded three at Belleville. That cultivated, critical city furnished Mr. Talmage the value of an audience in which professional men were predominant in influence. His preaching there grew tonic and free. As Mr. Pitt advised a young friend, he "risked himself." The church grew from few to many—from a state of coma to athletic life. The preacher learned to go to school to humanity and his own heart. The lessons they taught him agreed with what was boldest and most compelling in the spirit of the revealed Word. Those whose claims were sacred to him found the saline climate of Syracuse a cause of unhealth. Otherwise it is likely that that most delightful region in the United States—Central New York—for men of letters who equally love nature and culture, would have been the home of Mr. Talmage for life.

The next seven years of Mr. Talmage's life were spent in Philadelphia. There his powers got "set." He learned what it was he could best do. He had the courage of his consciousness and he did it. Previously he might have felt it incumbent on him to give to pulpit traditions the homage of compliance—though at Syracuse "the more excellent way," any man's *own* way, so that he have the divining gift of genius and the nature a-tune to all high sympathies and purposes—had in glimpses come to him. He realized that it was his duty and mission in the world to make *it* hear the gospel. The church was not to him in numbers a select few, in organization a monopoly. It was meant to be the conqueror and transformer of the world. For seven years he wrought with much success on this theory, all the time realizing that his plans could come to fullness only under conditions that enabled him to build from the bottom up an organization which could get nearer to the masses and which would have no precedents to be afraid of as ghosts in its path. Hence he ceased from being the leading preacher in Philadelphia to become in Brooklyn the leading preacher in the world.

His work for nine years here, know all our readers. It began in a cramped brick rectangle, capable of holding 1,200, and he came to it on "the call" of nineteen. In less than two years that was exchanged for an iron structure, with raised seats, the interior curved like a horse-shoe, the pulpit a platform bridging the ends. That held 3,000 persons. It lasted just long enough to revolutionize church architecture in cities into harmony with common sense. Smaller duplicates of it started in every quarter, three in Brooklyn, two in New York, one in Montreal, one in Louisville, any number in Chicago, two in San Francisco, like numbers abroad. Then it burnt up, that from its ashes the present stately and most sensible structure might rise. Gothic, of brick and stone, cathedral-like above, amphitheatre-like below, it holds 5,000 as easily as one person, and all can hear and see equally well. In a large sense the people built these edifices.

Their architects were Leonard Vaux and John Welch respectively. It is sufficiently indicative to say in general of Dr. Talmage's work in the Tabernacle, that his audiences are always as many as the place will hold; that twenty-three papers in Christendom statedly publish his entire sermons and Friday-night discourses, exclusive of the dailies of the United States; that the papers girdle the globe, being published in London, Liverpool, Manchester, Glasgow, Belfast, Toronto, Montreal, St. John's, Sidney, Melbourne, San Francisco, Chicago, Boston, Raleigh, New York, and many others. To pulpit labors of this responsibility should be added considerable pastoral work, the conduct of the Lay College, and constantly recurring lecturing and literary work, to fill out the public life of a very busy man.

The multiplicity, large results and striking progress of the labors of Dr. Talmage have made the foregoing more of a brief narrative of the epochs of his career than an account of the career itself. It has had to be so. Lack of space requires it. His work has had rather to be intimated in generalities than told in details. The filling in must come either from the knowledge of the reader or from intelligent inferences and conclusions, drawn from the few principal facts stated, and stated with care. This remains to be said: No other preacher addresses so many constantly. The words of no other preacher were ever before carried by so many types or carried so far. Types give him three continents for a church, and the English-speaking world for a congregation. The judgment of his generation will of course be divided upon him just as that of the next will not. That he is *a* topic in every newspaper is much more significant than the fact of what treatment it gives him. Only men of genius are universally commented on. The universality of the comment makes friends and foes alike prove the fact of the genius. That is what is impressive. As for the quality of the comment, it will, in nine cases out of ten, be much more a revelation of the character behind the pen which writes it than a true view or review of the man. This is necessarily so. The press and the pulpit in the main are defective judges of one another. The former rarely enters the inside of the latter's work. There is acquaintanceship, but not intimacy between them. Journals find out the *fact* of a preacher's power in time. Then they go looking for the causes Long before, however, the masses have felt the causes and have realized, not merely discovered, the fact. The penalty of being the leaders of great masses has, from Whitefield and Wesley to Spurgeon and Talmage, been to serve as the target for small wits. A constant source of attack on men of such magnitude always has been and will be the presses, which, by the common consent of mankind, are described and dispensed from all consideration, when they are rated Satanic. Their attacks confirm a man's right to respect and reputation, and are a proof of his influence and greatness. It can be truly said that while secular criticism in the United States favorably regards our subject in proportion to its intel ligence and uprightness, the judgment of foreigners on him has long been an index to the judgment of posterity here. No other American is read so much and so constantly abroad. His extraordinary imagination, earnestness, descriptive powers and humor, his great art in grouping and arrangement, his wonderful mastery of words to illumine and alleviate human conditions and to interpret and inspire the harmonies of the better nature, are appreciated by all who can put themselves in sympathy with his originality of methods and his high consecration of purpose. His manner mates with his nature. It is each sermon in action. He presses the eyes, hands, his entire body, into the service of the illustrative truth. Gestures are the accompaniment of what he says. As he stands out before the immense throng, without a scrap of notes or manuscript before him, the effect produced can not be understood by those who have never seen it. The solemnity, the tears, the awful hush, as though the audience could not breathe again, are oft-times painful.

His voice is peculiar, not musical, but productive of startling, strong effects, such as characterize no preacher on either side of the Atlantic. His power to grapple an audience and master it from text to peroration has no equal. No man was ever less self-conscious in his work. He feels a mission of evangelization on him as by the imposition of the Supreme. That mission he responds to by doing the duty that is nearest to him with all his might—as confident that he is under the care and order of a Divine Master as those who hear him are that they are under the spell of the greatest prose-poet that ever made the gospel his song and the redemption of the race the passion of his heart.

The following discourses were taken down by steno graphic reporters and revised by Mr. Talmage *specially for this work.* On the occasion of their delivery the church was thronged beyond description, the streets around blockaded with people so that carriages could not pass, Mr. Talmage himself gaining admission only by the help of the police.

CHAPTER I.

A PERSONAL EXPLORATION IN HAUNTS OF VICE.

"When said he unto me, Son of man, dig now in the wall; and when I had digged in the wall, behold a door. And he said unto me, Go in and behold the wicked abominations that they do here. So I went in and saw; and behold every form of creeping things and abominable beasts."—Ezekiel, viii: 8, 9, 10.

So this minister of religion, Ezekiel, was commanded to the exploration of the sin of his day. He was not to stand outside the door guessing what it was, but was to go in and see for himself. He did not in vision say: "O Lord, I don't wan't to go in; I dare not go in; if I go in I might be criticised; O Lord, please let me off?" When God told Ezekiel to go in he went in, "and saw, and behold all manner of creeping things and abominable beasts." I, as a minister of religion, felt I had a Divine commission to explore the iniquities of our cities. I did not ask counsel of my session, or my Presbytery, or of the newspapers, but asking the companionship of three prominent police officials and two of the elders of my church, I unrolled my commission, and it said: "Son of man, dig into the wall; and when I had digged into the wall, behold a door; and he said, Go in and see the wicked abominations that are done here; and I went in, and saw, and behold!" Brought up in the country and surrounded by much parental care, I had not until this autumn seen the haunts of iniquity. By the grace of God defended, I had never sowed any "wild oats." I had somehow been able to tell from various sources something about the iniquities of the great cities, and to preach against them; but I saw, in the destruction of a great multitude of the people, that there must be an infatuation and a temptation that had never been spoken about, and I said, "I will explore." I saw tens of thousands of men going down, and if there had been a spiritual percussion answering to the physical percussion, the whole air would have been full of the rumble, and roar, and crack, and thunder of the demolition, and this moment, if we should pause in our service, we should hear the crash, crash! Just as in the sickly season you sometimes hear the bell at the gate of the cemetery ringing almost incessantly, so I found that the bell at the gate of the cemetery where lost souls are buried was tolling by day and tolling by night. I said, "I will explore." I went as a physician goes into a small-pox hospital, or a fever lazzaretto, to see what practical and useful information I might get. That would be a foolish doctor who would stand outside the door of an invalid writing a Latin prescription. When the lecturer in a medical college is done with his lecture he takes the students into the dissecting room, and he shows them the reality. I am here this morning to report a plague, and to tell you how sin dissects the body, and dissects the mind, and dissects the soul. "Oh!" say you, "are you not afraid that in consequence of your exploration of the inquities of the city other persons may make exploration, and do themselves damage?" I reply: "If, in company with the Commissioner of Police, and the Captain of Police, and the Inspector of Police, and the company of two Christian gentlemen, and not with the spirit of curiosity, but that you may see sin in order the better to combat it, then, in the name of the eternal God, go? But, if not, then stay away. Wellington, standing in the battle of Waterloo when the bullets were buzzing around his head, saw a civilian on the field. He said to him, "Sir, what are you doing here? Be off?" "Why," replied the civilian, "there is no more danger here for me than there is for you." Then Wellington flushed up and said, "God and my country demand that I be here, but you have no errand here." Now I, as an officer in the army of Jesus Christ, went on this exploration, and on to this battle-field. If you bear a like commission, go; if not, stay away. But you say, "Don't you think that somehow your description of these places will induce people to go and see for themselves?" I answer, yes, just as much as the description of the yellow fever at Grenada would induce people to go down there and get the pestilence. It was told us there were hardly enough people alive to bury the dead, and I am going to tell you a story in these Sabbath morning sermons of places where they are all dead or dying. And I shall not gild iniquities. I shall play a dirge and not an anthem, and while I shall not put faintest blush on fairest cheek, I will kindle the cheeks of many a man into a conflagration, and I will make his ears tingle. But you say, "Don't you know that the papers are criticising you for the position you take?" I say, yes; and do you know how I feel about it! There is no man who is more indebted to the newspaper press than I am. My business is to preach the truth, and the wider the audience the newspaper press gives me, the wider my field is. As the secular and religious press of the United States and the Canadas, and of England and Ireland and Scotland and Australia and New Zealand, are giving me every week nearly three million souls for an audience, I say I am indebted to the press, anyhow. Go on! To the day of my death I cannot pay them what I owe them. So slash away, gentlemen. The more the merrier. If there is anything I despise, it is a dull time. Brisk criticism is a coarse Turkish towel, with which every public man needs every day to be rubbed down, in order to keep healthful circulation. Give my love to all the secular and religious editors, and full permission to run their steel pens clear through my sermons, from introduction to application.

It was ten o'clock of a calm, clear, star-lighted night when the carriage rolled with us from the bright part of the city down into the region where gambling and crime and death hold high carnival. When I speak of houses of dissipation, I do not refer to one sin, or five sins, but to all sins. As the horses halted, and, escorted by the officers of the law, we went in, we moved into a world of which we were as practically ignorant as though it had swung as far off from us as Mercury is from Saturn. No shout of revelry, no guffaw of laughter, but comparative silence. Not many signs of death, but the dead were there. As I moved through this place I said, "This is the home of lost souls." It was a Dante's Inferno; nothing to stir the mirth, but many things to fill the eyes with tears of pity. Ah! there were moral corpses. There were corpses on the stairway, corpses in the gallery, corpses in the gardens. Leper met leper, but no bandaged mouth kept back the breath. I felt that I was sitting on the iron coast against which Euroclydon had driven a hundred dismasted hulks—every moment more blackened hulks rolling in. And while I stood and waited for the going down of the storm and the lull of the sea, I bethought myself, this is an everlasting storm, and these billows always rage, and on each carcass that strewed the beach already had alighted a vulture—the long-beaked, filthy vulture of unending dispair—now picking into the corruption, and now on the black wing wiping the blood of a soul ! No lark, no robin, no chaffinch, but vultures, vultures, vultures. I was reading of an incident that occurred in Pennsylvania a few weeks ago, where a naturalist had presented to him a deadly serpent, and he put it in a bottle and stood it in his studio, and one evening, while in the studio with his daughter, a bat flew in the window, extinguished the light, struck the bottle containing the deadly serpent, and in a few moments there was a shriek from the daughter, and in a few hours she was dead. She had been bitten of the serpent. Amid these haunts of death, in that midnight exploration I saw that there were lions and eagles and doves for insignia; but I thought to myself how inappropriate. Better the insignia of an adder and a bat.

First of all, I have to report as a result of this midnight exploration that all the sacred rhetoric about the costly magnificence of the haunts of iniquity is apocryphal. We were shown what was called the costliest and most magnificent specimen. I had often heard that the walls were adorned with masterpieces; that the fountains were bewitching in the gaslight; that the music was like the touch of a Thalberg or a Gottschalk; that the upholstery was imperial; that the furniture in some places was like the throne-room of the Tuilleries. It is all false. Masterpieces! There was not a painting worth $5, leaving aside the frame. Great daubs of color that no intelligent mechanic would put on his wall. A crossbreed between a chromo and a splash of poor paint! Music! Some of the homeliest creatures I ever saw squawked discord, accompanied by pianos out of tune!

Upholstery! Two characteristics; red and cheap. You have heard so much about the wonderful lights—blue and green and yellow and orange flashing across the dancers and the gay groups. Seventy-five cents' worth of chemicals would produce all that in one night. Tinsel gewgaws, tawdriness frippery, seemingly much of it bought at a second-hand furniture store, and never paid for! For the most part, the inhabitants were repulsive. Here and there a soul on whom God had put the crown of beauty, but nothing comparable with the Christian loveliness and purity which you may see any pleasant afternoon on any of the thoroughfares of our great cities. Young man, you are a stark fool if you go to places of dissipation to see pictures, and hear music, and admire beautiful and gracious countenances. From Thomas's, or Dodworth's, or Gilmore's Band, in ten minutes you will hear more harmony than in a whole year of the racket and bang of the cheap orchestras of the dissolute. Come to me, and I will give you a letter of introduction to any one of five hundred homes in Brooklyn and New York, where you will see finer pictures and hear more beautiful music--music and pictures compared with which there is nothing worth speaking of in houses of dissipation. Sin, however pretentious, is almost always poor. Mirrors, divans, Chickering grand she cannot keep. The sheriff is after it with uplifted mallet, ready for the vendue. "Going! going! gone!

But, my friends, I noticed in all the haunts of dissipation that there was an attempt at music, however poor. The door swung open and shut to music; they stepped to music; they danced to music; they attempted nothing without music, and I said to myself, "If such inferior music has such power, and drum, and fife, and orchestra are enlisted in the service of the devil, what multipotent power there must be in music! and is it not high time that in all our churches and reform associations we tested how much charm there is in it to bring men off the wrong road to the right road?" Fifty times that night I said within myself, "If poor music is so powerful in a bad direction, why cannot good music be almost omnipotent in a good direction?" Oh! my friends, we want to drive men into the kingdom of God with a musical staff. We want to shut off the path of death with a musical bar. We want to snatch all the musical instruments from the service of the devil, and with organ, and cornet, and base viol, and piano and orchestra praise the Lord. Good Richard Cecil when seated in the pulpit, said that when Doctor Wargan was at the organ, he, Mr. Cecil, was so overpowered with the music that he found himself looking for the first chapter of Isaiah in the prayer book, wondering he could not find it. Oh! holy bewilderment. Let us send such men as Phillip Phillips, the Christian vocalist, all around the world, and Arbuckle, the cornest, with his "Robin Adair" set to Christian melody, and George Morgan with his Hallelujah Chorus, and ten thousand Christian men with uplifted hosannas to capture this whole earth for God. Oh! my friends, we have had enough minor strains in the church; give us major strains. We have had enough dead marches in the church; play us those tunes which are played when an army is on a dead run to overtake an enemy. Give us the double-quick. We are in full gallop of cavalry charge. Forward, the whole line! Many a man who is unmoved by Christian argument surrenders to a Christian song.

Many a man under the power of Christian music has had a change take place in his soul and in his life equal to that which took place in the life of a man in Scotland, who for fifteen years had been a drunkard. Coming home late at night, as he touched the doorsill, his wife trembled at his coming. Telling the story afterward, she said, "I didn't dare go to bed lest he violently drag me forth. When he came home there was only about the half inch of the candle left in the socket. When he entered, he said: 'Where are the children?' and I said, 'They are up stairs in bed.' He said, 'Go and fetch them,' and I went up and I knelt down and I prayed God to defend me and my children from their cruel father. And then I brought them down. He took up the eldest in his arms and kissed her and said, 'My dear lass, the Lord hath sent thee a father home to-night.' And so he did with the second, and then he took up the third of the children and said, 'My dear boy, the Lord hath sent thee home a father to-night.' And then he took up the babe and said, 'My darling babe, the Lord hath sent thee home a father to-night.' And then he put his arm around me and kissed me, and said, 'My dear lass, the Lord hath sent thee home a husband to-night.' Why, sir, I had na' heard anything like that for fourteen years. And he prayed and he was comforted, and my soul was restored, for I didn't live as I ought to have lived, close to God. My trouble had broken me down." Oh! for such a transformation in some of the homes of Brooklyn to-day. By holy conspiracy, in the last song of the morning, let us sweep every prodigal into the kingdom of our God. Oh! ye chanters above Bethlehem, come and hover this morning and give us a snatch of the old tune about "good will to men."

But I have, also to report of that midnight exploration, that I saw something that amazed me more than I can tell. I do not want to tell it, for it will take pain to many hearts far away, and I cannot comfort them. But I must tell it. In all these haunts of iniquity I found young men with the ruddy color of country health on their cheek, evidently just come to town for business, entering stores, and shops, and offices. They had helped gather the summer grain. There they were in haunts of iniquity, the look on their cheek which is never on the cheek except when there has been hard work on the farm and in the open air. Here were these young men who had heard how gayly a boat dances on the edge of a maelstrom, and they were venturing. O God! will a few weeks do such an awful work for a young man? O Lord! hast thou forgotten what transpired when they knelt at the family altar that morning when he came away, and how father's voice trembled in the prayer, and mother and sister sobbed as they lay on the floor? I saw that young man when he first confronted evil. I saw it was the first night there. I saw on him a defiant look, as much as to say, "I am mightier than sin." Then I saw him consult with iniquity. Then I saw him waver and doubt. Then I saw going over his countenance the shadow of sad reflections, and I knew from his looks there was a powerful memory stirring his soul. I think there was a whisper going out from the gaudy upholstery, saying, "My son, go home." I think there was a hand stretched out from under the curtains—a hand tremulous with anxiety, a hand that had been worn with work, a hand partly wrinkled with age, that seemed to beckon him away, and so goodness and sin seemed to struggle in that young man's soul; but sin triumphed, and he surrendered to darkness and to death—an ox to the slaughter. Oh! my soul, is this the end of all the good advice? Is this the end of all the prayers that have been made?

Have the clusters of the country vineyard been thrown into this great wine-press where Despair and Anguish and Death trample, and the vintage is a vintage of blood? I do not feel so sorry for that young man who, brought up in city life, knows beforehand what are all the surrounding temptations; but God pity the country lad unsuspecting and easily betrayed. Oh! young man from the farmhouse among the hills, what have your parents done that you should do this against them? Why are you bent on killing with trouble her who gave you birth? Look at her fingers—what makes them so distort? Working for you. Do you prefer to that honest old face the berouged cheek of sin? Write home to-morrow morning by the first mail, cursing your mother's white hair, cursing her stooped shoulder, cursing her old arm-chair, cursing the cradle in which she rocked you. "Oh!" you say, "I can't, I can't." You are doing it already. There is something on your hands, on your forehead, on your feet. It is red. What is it? The blood of a mother's broken heart! When you were threshing the harvest apples from that tree at the corner of the field last summer, did you think you would ever come to this? Did you think that the sharp sickle of death would cut you down so soon? If I thought I could break the infatuation I would come down from the pulpit and throw my arms around you and beg you to stop. Perhaps I am a little more sympathetic with such because I was a country lad. It was not until fifteen years of age that I saw a great city. I remember how stupendous New York looked as I arrived at Cortlandt Ferry. And now that I look back and remember that I had a nature all awake to hilarities and amusements, it is a wonder that I escaped. I was saying this to a gentleman in New York a few days ago, and he said, "Ah! sir, I guess there were some prayers hovering about." When I see a young man coming from the tame life of the country and going down in the city ruin, I am not surprised. My only surprise is that any escape, considering the allurements. I was a few days ago on the St. Lawrence river, and I said to the captain, "What a swift stream this is." "Oh!" he replied, "seventy-five miles from here it is ten times swifter. Why, we have to employ an Indian pilot, and we give him $1,000 for his summer's work, just to conduct our boats through between the rocks and the islands, so swift are the rapids." Well, my friends, every man that comes into New York and Brooklyn life comes into the rapids, and the only question is whether he shall have safe or unsafe pilotage. Young man, your bad habits will be reported at the homestead. You cannot hide them. There are people who love to carry bad news, and there will be some accursed old gossip who will wend her infernal step toward the old homestead, and she will sit down, and, after she has a while wriggled in the chair she will say to your old parents, "Do you know your son drinks?" Then your parents will get white about the lips, and your mother will ask to have the door set a little open for the fresh air, and before that old gossip leaves the place she will have told your parents all about the places where you are accustomed to go. Then your mother will come out, and she will sit down on the step where you used to play, and she will cry and cry. Then she will be sick, and the gig of the country doctor will come up the country lane, and the horse will be tied at the swing-gate, and the prescription will fail, and she will get worse and worse, and in her delirium she will talk about nothing but you. Then the farmers will come to the funeral, and tie the horses at the rail fence about the house, and they will talk about what ailed the one that died, and one will say it was intermittent, and another will say it was congestion, and another will say it was premature old age; but it will be neither intermittent, nor congestion, nor old age. In the ponderous book of Almighty God it will be recorded for everlasting ages to read that you killed her. Our language is very fertile in describing different kinds of crime. Slaying a man is homicide. Slaying a brother is fratricide. Slaying a father is patricide. Slaying a mother is matricide. It takes two words to describe your crime—patricide and matricide.

I must leave to other Sabbath mornings the unrolling of the scroll which I have this morning only laid on your table. We have come only to the vestibule of the subject. I have been treating of generals. I shall come to specifics. I have not told you of all the styles of people I saw in the haunts of iniquity. Before I get through with these sermons and next Sabbath morning I will answer the question everywhere asked me, why does municipal authority allow these haunts of iniquity?

I will show all the obstacles in the way. Sirs, before I get through with this course of Sabbath morning sermons, by the help of the eternal God, I will save ten thousand men! And in the execution of this mission I defy all earth and hell.

But I was going to tell you of an incident. I said to the officer, "Well, let us go; I am tired of this scene;" and as we passed out of the haunts of iniquity into the fresh air, a soul passed in. What a face that was! Sorrow only half covered up with an assumed joy. It was a woman's face. I saw as plainly as on the page of a book the tragedy. You know that there is such a thing as somnambulism, or walking in one's sleep. Well, in a fatal somnambulism, a soul started off from her father's house. It was very dark, and her feet were cut of the rocks; but on she went until she came to the verge of a chasm, and she began to descend from bowlder to bowlder down over the rattling shelving—for you know while walking in sleep people will go where they would not go when awake. Further on down, and further, where no owl of the night or hawk of the day would venture. On down until she touched the depth of the chasm. Then, in walking sleep, she began to ascend the other side of the chasm, rock above rock, as the roe boundeth. Without having her head to swim with the awful steep, she scaled the height. No eye but the sleepless eye of God watched her as she went down one side the chasm and came up the other side the chasm. It was an August night, and a storm was gathering, and a loud burst of thunder awoke her from her somnambulism, and she said, "Whither shall I fly?" and with an affrighted eye she looked back upon the chasm she had crossed, and she looked in front, and there was a deeper chasm before her. She said, "What shall I do? Must I die here?" And as she bent over the one chasm, she heard the sighing of the past; and as she bent over the other chasm, she heard the portents of the future. Then she sat down on the granite crag, and cried: "O! for my father's house! O! for the cottage, where I might die amid embowering honeysuckle! O! the past! O! the future! O! father! O! mother! O! God!" But the storm that had been gathering culminated, and wrote with finger of lightning on the sky just above the horizon, "The way of the transgressor is hard." And then thunder-peal after thunder-peal uttered it: "Which forsaketh the guide of her youth and forgetteth the covenant of her God. Destroyed without remedy!" And the cavern behind echoed it, "Destroyed without remedy!" And the chasm before echoed it, "Destroyed without remedy!" There she perished, her cut and bleeding feet on the edge of one chasm, her long locks washed of the storm dripping over the other chasm.

But by this time our carriage had reached the curbstone of my dwelling, and I awoke, and behold it was a dream!

CHAPTER II.

THE LEPERS OF HIGH LIFE.

"Policeman, what of the night?"—Isaiah xxi: 11.

The original of the text may be translated either "watchman" or "policeman." I have chosen the latter word. The olden-time cities were all thus guarded. There were roughs, and thugs, and desperadoes in Jerusalem, as well as there are in New York and Brooklyn. The police headquarters of olden time was on top of the city wall. King Solomon, walking incognito through the streets, reports in one of his songs that he met these officials. King Solomon must have had a large posse of police to look after his royal grounds, for he had twelve thousand blooded horses in his stables, and he had millions of dollars in his palace, and he had six hundred wives, and, though the palace was large, no house was ever large enough to hold two women married to the same man; much less could six hundred keep the peace. Well, the night was divided into three watches, the first watch reaching from sundown to 10 o'clock; the second watch from 10 o'clock to two in the morning; the third watch from two in the morning to sunrise. An Idumean, anxious about the prosperity of the city, and in regard to any danger that might threaten it, accosts an officer just as you might any night upon our streets, saying, "Policeman, what of the night?" Policemen, more than any other people, understand a city. Upon them are vast responsibilities for small pay. The police officer of your city gets $1,100 salary, but he may spend only one night of an entire month in his family. The detective of your city gets $1,500 salary, but from January to January there is not an hour that he may call his own. Amid cold and heat and tempest, and amid the perils of the bludgeon of the midnight assassin, he does his work. The moon looks down upon nine-tenths of the iniquity of our great cities. What wonder, then, that a few weeks ago, in the interest of morality and religion, I asked the question of the text, "Policeman, what of the night?" In addition to this powerful escortage, I asked two elders of the church to accompany me; not because they were any better than the other elders of the church, but because they were more muscular, and I was resolved that in any case where anything more than spiritual defense was necessary, to refer the whole matter to their hands! I believe in muscular Christianity. I wish that our theological seminaries, instead of sending out so many men with dyspepsia and liver complaint and all out of breath by the time they have climbed to the top of the pulpit stairs, would, through gymnasiums and other means, send into the pulpit physical giants as well as spiritual athletes. I do wish I could consecrate to the Lord two hundred and fifty pounds avoirdupois weight? But, borrowing the strength of others, I started out on the midnight exploration. I was preceded in this work by Thomas Chalmers, who opened every door of iniquity in Edinburgh before he established systematic amelioration, and preceded by Thomas Guthrie, who explored all the squalor of the city before he established the ragged schools, and by every man who has done anything to balk crime, and help the tempted and the destroyed. Above all, I followed in the footsteps of Him who was derided by the hypocrites and the sanhedrims of his day, because he persisted in exploring the deepest moral slush of his time, going down among demoniacs and paupers and adulteresses, never so happy as when he had ten lepers to cure. Some of you may have been surprised that there was a great hue and cry raised before these sermons were begun, and sometimes the hue and cry was made by professors of religion. I was not surprised. The simple fact is that in all our churches there are lepers who do not want their scabs touched, and they foresaw that before I got through with this series of sermons I would show up some of the wickedness and rottenness of what is called the upper class. The devil howled because he knew I was going to hit him hard! Now, I say to all such men, whether in the church or out of it, "Ye hypocrites, ye generation of vipers, how can ye escape the damnation of hell?"

I noticed in my midnight exploration with these high officials that the haunts of sin are chiefly supported by men of means and men of wealth. The young men recently come from the country, of whom I spoke last Sabbath morning, are on small salary, and they have but little money to spend in sin, and if they go into luxuriant iniquity the employer finds it out by the inflamed eye and the marks of dissipation, and they are discharged. The luxuriant places of iniquity are supported by men, who come down from the fashionable avenues of New York, and cross over from some of the finest mansions of Brooklyn. Prominent business men from Boston, Philadelphia, and Chicago, and Cincinnati, patronize these places of crime. I could call the names of prominent men in our cluster of cities who patronize these places of iniquity, and I may call their names before I get through this course of sermons, though the fabric of New York and Brooklyn society tumble into wreck. Judges of courts, distinguished lawyers, officers of the church, political orators standing on Republican and Democratic and Greenback platforms talking about God and good morals until you might suppose them to be evangelists expecting a thousand converts in one night. Call the roll of dissipation in the haunts of iniquity any night, and if the inmates will answer, you will find there stock-brokers from Wall street, large importers from Broadway, iron merchants, leather merchants, cotton merchants, hardware merchants, wholesale grocers, representatives from all the commercial and wealthy classes. Talk about the heathenism below Canal street! There is a worse heathenism above Canal street. I prefer that kind of heathenism which wallows in filth and disgusts the beholder rather than that heathenism which covers up its walking putrefaction with camel's-hair shawl and point lace, and rides in turnouts worth $3,000, liveried driver ahead and rosetted flunky behind. We have been talking so much about the gospel for the masses; now let us talk a little about the gospel for the lepers of society, for the millionaire sots, for the portable lazzarettos of upper-tendom. It is the iniquity that comes down from the higher circles of society that supports the haunts of crime, and it is gradually turning our cities into Sodoms and Gomorrahs waiting for the fire and brimstone tempest of the Lord God who whelmed the cities of the plain. We want about five hundred Anthony Comstocks to go forth and explore and expose the abominations of high life. For eight or ten years there stood within sight of the most fashionable New York drive a Moloch temple, a brown-stone hell on earth, which neither the Mayor, nor the judges, nor the police dared touch, when Anthony Comstock, a Christian man of less than average physical stature, and with cheek scarred by the knife of a desperado whom he had arrested, walked into that palace of the damned on Fifth avenue, and in the name of God put an end to to it, the priestess presiding at the orgies retreating by suicide into the lost world, her bleeding corpse found in her own bath-tub. May the eternal God have mercy on our cities. Gilded sin comes down from these high places into the upper circles of iniquity, and then on gradually down, until in five years it makes the whole pilgrimage, from the marble pillar on the brilliant avenue clear down to the cellars of Water street. The officer on that midnight exploration said to me: "Look at them now, and look at them three years from now when all this glory has departed; they'll be a heap of rags in the station house." Another of the officers said to me: "That is the daughter of one of the wealthiest families on Madison square."

But I have something more amazing to tell you than that the men of means and wealth support these haunts of iniquity, and that is, that they are chiefly supported by heads of families—fathers and husbands, with the awful perjury of broken marriage vows upon them, with a niggardly stipend left at home for the support of their families, going forth with their thousands for the diamonds and wardrobe and equipage of iniquity. In the name of heaven, I denounce this public iniquity. Let such men be hurled out of decent circles. Let them be hurled out from business circles. If they will not repent, overboard with them! I lift one-half the burden of malediction from the unpitied head of offending woman, and hurl it on the blasted pate of offending man! Society needs a new division of its anathema. By what law of justice does burning excoriation pursue offending woman down off the precipices of destruction, while offending man, kid-gloved, walks in refined circles, invited up if he have money, advanced into political recognition, while all the doors of high life open at the first rap of his gold-headed cane? I say, if you let one come back, let them both come back. If one must go down, let both go down. I give you as my opinion that the eternal perdition of all other sinners will be a heaven compared with the punishment everlasting of that man who, turning his back upon her whom he swore to protect and defend until death, and upon his children, whose destiny may be decided by his example, goes forth to seek affectional alliances elsewhere. For such a man the portion will be fire, and hail, and tempest, and darkness, and blood, and anguish, and despair forever, forever, forever! My friends, there has got to be a reform in this matter, or American society will go to pieces. Under the head of "incompatibility of temper," nine-tenths of the abomination goes on. What did you get married for if your dispositions are incompatible? "Oh!" you say, "I rushed into it without thought" Then you ought to be willing to suffer the punishment for making a fool of yourself! Incompatibility of temper! You are responsible for at least a half of the incompatibility Why are you not honest and willing to admit either that you did not control your temper, or that you had already broken your marriage oath? In nine hundred and ninety-nine cases out of the thousand, incompatibility is a phrase to cover up wickedness already enacted. I declare in the presence of this city and in the presence of the world that heads of families are supporting these haunts of iniquity. I wish there might be a police raid lasting a great while, that they would just go down through all these places of sin and gather up all the prominent business men of the city, and march them down through the street followed by about twenty reporters to take their names and put them in full capitals in the next day's paper! Let such a course be undertaken in our cities, and in six months there would be eighty per cent. off your public crime. It is not now the young men and the boys that need so much looking after; it is their fathers and mothers. Let heads of families cease to patronize places of iniquity, and in a short time they would crumble to ruin.

But you meet me with the question, "Why don't the city authorities put an end to such places of iniquity?" I answer in regard to Brooklyn, the work has already been done. Six years ago there were in the radius of your City Hall thirty-eight gambling saloons. They are all broken up. The ivory and wooden "chips" that came from the gambling-hells into the Police Headquarters came in by the peck. How many inducements were offered to our officials, such as: "This will be worth a thousand dollars to you if you will let it go on." "This will be worth five thousand if you will only let it go on." But our commissioners of police, mightier than any bribe, pursued their work until, while beyond the city limits there may be exceptions, within the city limits of Brooklyn there is not a gambling-hell, or policy-shop, or a house of death so pronounced. There are underground iniquities and hidden scenes, but none so pronounced. Every Monday morning all the captains of the police make reports in regard to their respective precincts. When the work began, the police in authority at that time said: "Oh! it can't be done; we can't get into these places of iniquity to see them, and hence we can't break them up." "Then," said the commissioners of police, "break in the doors;" and it is astonishing how soon after the shoulders of a stout policeman goes against the door, it gets off its hinges. Some of the captains of police said: "This thing has been going on so long, it cannot be crushed." "Then," said the commissioners of police, "we'll get other captains of police." The work went on until now, if a reformer wants the commissioners of police to show him the haunts of iniquity in Brooklyn, there are none to show him. If you know a single case that is an exception to what I say, report it to me at the close of this service at the foot of this platform, and I will warrant that within two hours after you report the case Commissioner Jourdan, Superintendent Campbell, Inspector Waddy, and as many of the twenty-five detectives and of the five hundred and fifty policemen as are necessary will come down on it like an Alpine avalanche. If you do not report it, it is because you are a coward, or else because you are in the sin yourself, and you do not want it shown up. You shall bear the whole responsibility, and it shall not be thrown on the hard-working and heroic detective and police force. But you say: "How has this general clearing out of gambling-hells and places of iniquity been accomplished?" Our authorities have been backed up by a high public sentiment. In a city which has on its judicial bench such magnificent men as Neilson, and Reynolds, and McCue, and Moore, and Pratt, and others whom I am not fortunate enough to know, there must be a mighty impulse upward toward God and good morals. We have in the high places of this city men not only with great heads, but with great hearts. A young man disappeared from his father's house about the time the Brooklyn Theater burned, and it was supposed that he had been destroyed in that ruin. The father, broken-hearted, sold his property in Brooklyn, and in desolation left the city. Recently the wandering son came back. He could not find his father, who, in departing, had given no idea of his destination. The case was reported to a man high in official position, and he sat down and wrote a letter to all the chiefs of police in the United States, in order that he might deliver that prodigal son into the arms of his broken-hearted father. A few days ago it was found that the father was in California. I understand that son is now on the way to meet him, and it will be the parable of the prodigal son over again when they embrace each other, and the father says: "Rejoice with me, for this my son was dead and is alive again, was lost and is found." I have forgotten the name of the father, I have forgotten the name of his son; but I have not forgotten the name of the officer whose sympathetic heart beats so loud under his badge of office. It was Patrick Campbell, Superintendent of the Brooklyn police. I do not mention these things as a matter of city pride, nor as a matter of exultation, but of gratitude to God that Brooklyn to-day stands foremost among American cities in its freedom from places of iniquity. But Brooklyn has a large share of sin. Where do the people of Brooklyn go when they propose to commit abomination? To New York. I was told in the midnight exploration in New York with the police that there are some places almost entirely supported by men and women from Brooklyn. We are one city after all—one now before the bridge is completed, to be more thoroughly one when the bridge is done.

Well, then, you press me with another question: "Why don't the public authorities of New York extirpate these haunts of iniquity?" Before I give you a definite answer I want to say that the obstacles in that city are greater than in any city on this continent. It is so vast. It is the landing-place of European immigration. Its wealth is mighty to establish and defend places of iniquity. Twice a year there are incursions of people from all parts of the land coming on the spring and the fall trade. It requires twenty times the municipal energy to keep order in New York that it does in any city from Portland to San Francisco. But still you pursue me with the question, and I am to answer it by telling you that there is infinite fault and immensity of blame to be divided between three parties. First, the police of New York city. So far as I know them they are courteous gentlemen. They have had great discouragement, they tell me, in the fact that when they arrest crime and bring it before the courts the witnesses will not appear lest they criminate themselves. They tell me also that they have been discouraged by the fact that so many suits have been brought against them for damages. But after all, my friends, they must take their share of blame. I have come to the conclusion, after much research and investigation, that there are captains of police in New York who are in complicity with crime—men who make thousands of dollars a year for the simple fact that they will not tell, and will permit places of iniquity to stand month after month, and year after year. I am told that there are captains of police in New York who get a percentage on every bottle of wine sold in the haunts of death, and that they get a revenue from all the shambles of sin. What a state of things this is! In the Twenty-ninth precinct of New York there are one hundred and twenty-one dens of death. Night after night, month after month, year after year, untouched. In West Twenty-sixth street and West Twenty-seventh street and West Thirty-first street there are whole blocks that are a pandemonium. There are between five and six hunared dens of darkness in the city of New York, where there are 2,500 policemen. Not long ago there was a masquerade ball in which the masculine and feminine offenders of society were the participants, and some of the police danced in the masquerade and distributed the prizes! There is the grandest opportunity that has ever opened, for any American, open now. It is for that man in high official position who shall get into his stirrups and say, "Men, follow?" and who shall in one night sweep around and take all of these leaders of iniquity, whether on suspicion or on positive proof, saying, "I'll take the responsibility, come on! I put my private property and my political aspirations and my life into this crusade against the powers of darkness." That man would be Mayor of the city of New York. That man would be fit to be President of the United States.

But the second part of the blame I must put at the door of the District Attorney of New York. I understand he is an honorable gentleman, but he has not time to attend to all these cases. Literally, there are thousands of cases unpursued for lack of time. Now, I say, it is the business of New York to give assistants, and clerks, and help to the District Attorney until all these places shall go down in quick retribution.

But the third part of the blame, and the heaviest part of it, I put on the moral and Christian people of our cities, who are guilty of most culpable indifference on this whole subject. When Tweed stole his millions large audiences were assembled in indignation, Charles O'Conor was retained, committees of safety and investigation were appointed, and a great stir made; but night by night there is a theft and a burglary of city morals as much worse than Tweed's robberies as his were worse than common shop-lifting, and it has very little opposition. I tell you what New York wants; it wants indignation meetings in Cooper Institute and Academy of Music and Chickering and Irving Halls to compel the public authorities to do their work and to send the police, with clubs and lanterns and revolvers, to turn off the colored lights of the dance-houses, and to mark for confiscation the trunks and wardrobes and furniture and scenery, and to gather up all the keepers, and all the inmates, and all the patrons, and march them out to the Tombs, fife and drum sounding the Rogue's March.

While there are men smoking their cigarettes, with their feet on Turkish divans, shocked that a minister of religion should explore and expose the iniquity of city life, there are raging underneath our great cities a Cotopaxi, a Stromboli, a Vesuvius, ready to bury us in ashes and scoria deeper than that which overwhelmed Pompeii and Herculaneum. Oh! I wish the time would come for the plowshare of public indignation to push through and rip up and turn under those parts of New York which are the plague of the nation. Now is the time to hitch up the team to this plowshare. In this time, when Mr. Cooper is Mayor, and Mr. Kelly is Comptroller, and Mr. Nichols is Police Commissioner, and Superintendent Walling wears the badge of office, and there is on the judicial benches of New York an array of the best men that have ever occupied those positions since the foundation of the city—Recorder Hackett, Police Magistrates Kilbreth, Wandell, Morgan and Duffy; such men as Gildersleeve, and Sutherland, and Davis, and Curtis; and on the United States Court bench in New York such men as Benedict, and Blatchford, and Choate—now is the time to make an extirpation of iniquity. Now is the time for a great crusade, and for the people of our cities in great public assemblages to say to police authority:

"Go ahead, and we will back you with our lives, our fortunes, and our sacred honor."

I must adjourn until next Sabbath morning much of what I wanted to say about certain forms of iniquity which I saw rampant in the night of my exploration with the city officials. But before I stop this morning I want to have one word with a class of men with whom people have so little patience that they never get a kind word of invitation. I mean the men who have forsaken their homes. Oh! my brother, return. You say: "I can't; I have no home; my home is broken up." Re-establish your home. It has been done in other cases, why may it not be done in your case? "Oh," you say, "we parted for life; we have divided our property; we have divided our effects." I ask you, did you divide the marriage ring of that bright day when you started life together? Did you divide your family Bible? If so, where did you divide it? Across the Old Testament, where the Ten Commandments denounce your sin, or across the New Testament, where Christ says: "Blessed are the pure in heart?" Or did you divide it between the Old and the New Testaments, right across the family record of weddings and births and deaths? Did you divide the cradle in which you rocked your first born? Did you divide the little grave in the cemetery, over which you stood with linked arms, looking down in awful bereavement? Above all, I ask you, did you divide your hope for heaven, so that there is no full hope left for either of you? Go back! There may be a great gulf between you and once happy domesticity; but Christ will bridge that gulf. It may be a bridge of sighs. Turn toward it. Put your foot on the over-arching span. Hear it! It is a voice unrolling from the throne: "He that overcometh shall inherit all things, and I will be unto him a God, and he shall be my son; but the unbelieving, and the sorcerers, and the whoremongers, and the adulterers, and the idolators, and all liars shall have their part in the lake which burneth with fire and brimstone—which is the second death!"

CHAPTER III.

THE GATES OF HELL.

"The gates of hell shall not prevail against it."–St. Matthew xvi: 18.

"It is only 10 o'clock," said the officer of the law, as we got into the carriage for the midnight exploration—"it is only 10 o'clock, and it is too early to see the places that we wish to see, for the theaters have not yet let out." I said, "What do you mean by that?" "Well," he said, "the places of iniquity are not in full blast until the people have time to arrive from the theaters." So we loitered on, and the officer told the driver to stop on a street where is one of the costliest and most brilliant gambling-houses in the city of New York. As we came up in front all seemed dark. The blinds were down; the door was guarded; but after a whispering of the officer with the guard at the door, we were admitted into the hall, and thence into the parlors, around one table finding eight or ten men in mid-life, well-dressed—all the work going on in silence, save the noise of the rattling "chips" on the gaming-table in one parlor, and the revolving ball of the roulette table in the other parlor. Some of these men, we were told, had served terms in prison; some were ship-wrecked bankers and brokers and money-dealers, and some were going their first rounds of vice—but all intent upon the table, as large or small fortunes moved up and down before them. Oh! there was something awfully solemn in the silence—the intense gaze, the suppressed emotion of the players. No one looked up. They all had money in the rapids, and I have no doubt some saw, as they sat there, horses and carriages, and houses and lands, and home and family rushing down into the vortex. A man's life would not have been worth a farthing in that presence had he not been accompanied by the police, if he had been supposed to be on a Christian errand of observation. Some of these men went by private key, some went in by careful introduction, some were taken in by the patrons of the establishment. The officer of the law told me: "None get in here except by police m ndate, or by some letter of a patron." While we were there a young man came in, put his money down on the roulette-table, and lost; put more money down on the roulette-table, and lost; put more money down on the roulette-table, and lost; then feeling in his pockets for more money, finding none, in severe silence he turned his back upon the scene and passed out. All the literature about the costly magnificence of such places is untrue. Men kept their hats on and smoked, and there was nothing in the upholstery or the furniture to forbid. While we stood there men lost their property and lost their souls. Oh! merciless place. Not once in all the history of that gaming-house has there been one word of sympathy uttered for the losers at the game. Sir Horace Walpole said that a man dropped dead in front of one of the club-houses of London; his body was carried into the club-house, and the members of the club began immediately to bet as to whether he were dead or alive, and when it was proposed to test the matter by bleeding him, it was only hindered by the suggestion that it would be unfair to some of the players! In these gaming-houses of our cities, men have their property wrung away from them, and then they go out, some of them to drown their grief in strong drink, some to ply the counterfeiter's pen, and so restore their fortunes, some resort to the suicide's revolver, but all going down, and that work proceeds day by day, and night by night, until it is estimated that every day in Christendom eighty million dollars pass from hand to hand through gambling practices, and every year in Christendom one hundred and twenty-three billion, one hundred million dollars change hands in that way.

"But," I said, "it is 11 o'clock, and we must be off." We passed out into the hallway and so into the street, the burly guard slamming the door of the house after us, and we got into the carriage and rolled on toward the gates of hell. You know about the gates of heaven. You have often heard them preached about. There are three to each point of the compass. On the north, three gates; on the south, three gates; on the east, three gates; on the west, three gates; and each gate is of solid pearl. Oh! gate of heaven; may we all get into it. But who shall describe the gates of hell spoken of in my text? These gates are burnished until they sparkle and glisten in the gas-light. They are mighty, and set in sockets of deep and dreadful masonry. They are high, so that those who are in may not clamber over and get out. They are heavy, but they swing easily in to let those go in who are to be destroyed. Well, my friends, it is always safe to go where God tells you to go, and God had told me to go through these gates of hell, and explore and report, and, taking three of the high police authorities and two of the elders of my church, I went in, and I am here this morning to sketch the gates of hell. I remember, when the Franco-German war was going on, that I stood one day in Paris looking at the gates of the Tuilleries, and I was so absorbed in the sculpturing at the top of the gates—the masonry and the bronze—that I forgot myself, and after awhile, looking down, I saw that there were officers of the law scrutinizing me, supposing, no doubt, I was a German, and looking at those gates for adverse purposes. But, my friends, we shall not stand looking at the outside of the gates of hell. Through this midnight exploration I shall tell you of both sides, and I shall tell you what those gates are made of. With the hammer of God's truth I shall pound on the brazen panels, and with the lantern of God's truth I shall flash a light upon the shining hinges.

Gate the first: Impure literature. Anthony Comstock seized twenty tons of bad books, plates, and letter-press, and when our Professor Cochran, of the Polytechnic Institute, poured the destructive acids on those plates, they smoked in the righteous annihilation. And yet a great deal of the bad literature of the day is not gripped of the law. It is strewn in your parlors; it is in your libraries. Some of your children read it at night after they have retired, the gas-burner swung as near as possible to their pillow. Much of this literature is under the title of scientific information. A book agent with one of these infernal books, glossed over with scientific nomenclature, went into a hotel and sold in one day a hundred copies, and sold them all to women! It is appalling that men and women who can get through their family physician all the useful information they may need, and without any contamination, should wade chin deep through such accursed literature under the plea of getting useful knowledge, and that printing-presses, hoping to be called decent, lend themselves to this infamy. Fathers and mothers, be not deceived by the title, "medical works." Nine-tenths of those books come hot from the lost world, though they may have on them the names of the publishing-houses of New York and Philadelphia. Then there is all the novelette literature of the day flung over the land by the million. As there are good novels that are long, so I suppose there may be good novels that are short, and so there may be a good novelette, but it is the exception. No one—mark this--no one systematically reads the average novelette of this day and keeps either integrity or virtue. The most of these novelettes are written by broken-down literary men for small compensation, on the principle that, having failed in literature elevated and pure, they hope to succeed in the tainted and the nasty. Oh! this is a wide gate of hell. Every panel is made out of a bad book or newspaper. Every hinge is the interjoined type of a corrupt printing-press. Every bolt or lock of that gate is made out of the plate of an unclean pictorial. In other words, there are a million men and women in the United States to-day reading themselves into hell! When in your own beautiful city a prosperous family fell into ruins through the misdeeds of one of its members, the amazed mother said to the officer of the law: "Why, I never supposed there was anything wrong. I never thought there could be anything wrong." Then she sat weeping in silence for some time, and said: "Oh! I have got it now! I know, I now! I found in her bureau after she went away a bad book. That's what slew her." These leprous booksellers have gathered up the catalogues of all the male and female seminaries in the United States, catalogues containing the names and the residences of all the students, and circulars of death are sent to every one, without any exception. Can you imagine anything more deathful? There is not a young person, male or female, or an old person, who has not had offered to him or her a bad book or a bad picture.

Scour your house to find out whether there are any of these adders coiled on your parlor center-table, or coiled amid the toilet set on the dressing-case. I adjure you before the sun goes down to explore your family libraries with an inexorable scrutiny. Remember that one bad book or bad picture may do the work for eternity. I want to arouse all your suspicions about novelettes. I want to put you on the watch against everything that may seem like surreptitious correspondence through the postoffice. I want you to understand that impure literature is one of the broadest, highest, mightiest gates of the lost.

Gate the second: The dissolute dance. You shall not divert me to the general subject of dancing. Whatever you may think of the parlor dance, or the methodic motion of the body to sounds of music in the family or the social circle, I am not now discussing that question. I want you to unite with me this morning in recognizing the fact that there is a dissolute dance. You know of what I speak. It is seen not only in the low haunts of death, but in elegant mansions. It is the first step to eternal ruin for a great multitude of both sexes. You know, my friends, what postures, and attitudes, and figures are suggested of the devil. They who glide into the dissolute dance glide over an inclined plane, and the dance is swifter and swifter, wilder and wilder, until with the speed of lightning they whirl off the edges of a decent life into a fiery future. This gate of hell swings across the Axminster of many a fine parlor, and across the ball-room of the summer watering-place. You have no right, my brother, my sister—you have no right to take an attitude to the sound of music which would be unbecoming in the absence of music. No Chickering grand of city parlor or fiddle of mountain picnic can consecrate that which God hath cursed.

Gate the third: Indiscreet apparel. The attire of woman for the last four or five years has been beautiful and graceful beyond anything I have known; but there are those who will always carry that which is right into the extraordinary and indiscreet. I am told that there is a fashion about to come in upon us that is shocking to all righteousness. I charge Christian women, neither by style of dress nor adjustment of apparel, to become administrative of evil. Perhaps none else will dare to tell you, so I will tell you that there are multitudes of men who owe their eternal damnation to the boldness of womanly attire. Show me the fashion-plates of any age between this and the time of Louis XVI., of France, and Henry VIII., of England, and I will tell you the type of morals or immorals of that age or that year. No exception to it. Modest apparel means a righteous people. Immodest apparel always means a contaminated and depraved society. You wonder that the city of Tyre was destroyed with such a terrible destruction. Have you ever seen the fashion-plate of the city of Tyre? I will show it to you:

"Moreover, the Lord saith, because the daughters of Zion are haughty and walk with stretched-forth necks and wanton eyes, walking and mincing as they go, and making a tinkling with their feet, in that day the Lord will take away the bravery of their tinkling ornaments about their feet, and their cauls, and their round tires like the moon, the rings and nose jewels, the changeable suits of apparel, and the mantles, and the wimples, and the crisping-pins."

That is the fashion-plate of ancient Tyre. And do you wonder that the Lord God in His indignation blotted out the city, so that fishermen to-day spread their nets where that city once stood?

Gate the fourth: Alcoholic beverage. In our midnight exploration we saw that all the scenes of wickedness were under the enchantment of the wine-cup. That was what the waitresses carried on the platter. That was what glowed on the table. That was what shone in illuminated gardens. That was what flushed the cheeks of the patrons who came in. That was what staggered the step of the patrons as they went out. Oh! the wine-cup is the patron of impurity. The officers of the law that night told us that nearly all the men who go into the shambles of death go in intoxicated, the mental and the spiritual abolished, that the brute may triumph. Tell me that a young man drinks, and I know the whole story. If he become a captive of the wine-cup, he will become a captive of all other vices; only give him time. No one ever runs drunkenness alone. That is a carrion-crow that goes in a flock, and when you see that beak ahead, you may know the other beaks are coming. In other words, the wine-cup unbalances and dethrones one's better judgment, and leaves one the prey of all evil appetites that may choose to alight upon his soul. There is not a place of any kind of sin in the United States to-day that does not find its chief abettor in the chalice of inebriacy. There is either a drinking-bar before, or one behind, or one above, or one underneath. The officers of the law said to me that night: "These people escape legal penalty because they are all licensed to sell liquor." Then I said within myself, "The courts that license the sale of strong drink, license gambling-houses, license libertinism, license disease, license death, license all sufferings, all crimes, all despoliations, all disasters, all murders, all woe. It is the courts and the Legislature that are swinging wide open this grinding, creaky, stupendous gate of the lost."

But you say, "You have described these gates of hell and shown us how they swing in to allow the entrance of the doomed. Will you not, please, before you get through the sermon, tell us how these gates of hell may swing out to allow the escape of the penitent?" I reply, but very few escape. Of the thousand that go in nine hundred and ninety-nine perish. Suppose one of these wanderers should knock at your door, would you admit her? Suppose you knew where she came from, would you ask her to sit down at your dining-table? Would you ask her to become the governess of your children? Would you introduce her among your acquaintanceships? Would you take the responsibility of pulling on the outside of the gate of hell while she pushed on the inside of that gate trying to get out? You would not, not one of a thousand of you that would dare to do it. You write beautiful poetry over her sorrows and weep over her misfortunes, but give her practical help you never will. There is not one person out of a thousand that will—there is not one out of five thousand that has—come so near the heart of the Lord Jesus Christ as to dare to help one of these fallen souls. But you say, "Are there no ways by which the wanderer may escape?" Oh, yes; three or four. The one way is the sewing-girl's garret, dingy, cold, hunger-blasted. But you say, "Is there no other way for her to escape?" Oh, yes. Another way is the street that leads to the East river, at midnight, the end of the city dock, the moon shining down on the water making it look so smooth she wonders if it is deep enough. It is. No boatman near enough to hear the plunge. No watchman near enough to pick her out before she sinks the third time. No other way? Yes. By the curve of the Hudson River Railroad at the point where the engineer of the lightning express train cannot see a hundred yards ahead to the form that lies across the track. He may whistle "down brakes," but not soon enough to disappoint the one who seeks her death. But you say, "Isn't God good, and won't he forgive?" Yes; but man will not, woman will not, society will not. The church of God says it will, but it will not. Our work, then, must be prevention rather than cure. Standing here telling this story to-day, it is not so much in the hope that I will persuade one who has dashed down a thousand feet over the rocks to crawl up again into life and light, but it is to alarm those who are coming too near the edges. Have you ever listened to hear the lamentation that rings up from those far depths?

> "Once I was pure as the snow, but I fell,
> Fell like a snowflake, from heaven to hell;
> Fell, to be trampled as filth of the street;
> Fell, to be scoffed at, be spit on, and beat.
> Pleading, cursing, begging to die,
> Selling my soul to whoever would buy;
> Dealing in shame for a morsel of bread,
> Hating the living and fearing the dead."

But you say. "What can be the practical use of this course of sermons?" I say, much everywhere. I am greatly obliged to those gentlemen of the press who have fairly reported what I have said on these occasions, and the press of this city and New York, and of the other prominent cities. I thank you for the almost universal fairness with which you have presented what I have had to say. Of course, among the educated and refined journalists who sit at these tables, and have been sitting here for four or five years, there will be a fool or two that does not understand his business, but that ought not to discredit the grand newspaper printing-press. I thank also, those who have by letters cheered me in this work—letters coming from all parts of the land, from Christian reformers telling me to go on in the work which I have undertaken. Never so many letters in my life have I received. Perhaps one out of the hundred condemnatory, as one I got yesterday from a man who said he thought my sermons would do great damage in the fact that they would arouse the suspicion of domestic circles as to where the head of the family was spending his evenings! I was sorry it was an anonymous letter, for I should have written to that man's wife telling her to put a detective on her husband's track, for I knew right away he was going to bad places! My friends, you say, "It is not possible to do anything with these stalwart iniquities; you cannot wrestle them down." Stupid man, read my text: "The gates of hell shall not prevail against the church." Those gates of hell are to be prostrated just as certainly as God and the Bible are true, but it will not be done until Christian men and women, quitting their prudery and squeamishness in this matter, rally the whole Christian sentiment of the church and assail these great evils of society. The Bible utters its denunciation in this direction again and again, and yet the piety of the day is such a namby-pamby, emetic sort of a thing that you cannot even quote Scripture without making somebody restless. As long as this holy imbecility reigns in the church of God, sin will laugh you to scorn. I do not know but that before the church wakes up matters will get worse and worse, and that there will have to be one lamb sacrificed from each of the most carefully-guarded folds, and the wave of uncleanness dash to the spire of the village church and the top of the cathedral pillar. Prophets and patriarchs, and apostles and evangelists,and Christ himself have thundered against these sins as against no other, and yet there are those who think we ought to take, when we speak of these subjects, a tone apologetic. I put my foot on all the conventional rhetoric on this subject, and I tell you plainly that unless you give up that sin your doom is sealed, and world without end you will be chased by the anathemas of an incensed God. I rally you under the cheerful prophecy of the text; I rally you to a besiegement of the gates of hell. We want in this besieging host no soft sentimentalists, but men who are willing to give and take hard knocks. The gates of Gaza were carried off, the gates of Thebes were battered down, the gates of Babylon were destroyed, and the gates of hell are going to be prostrated. The Christianized printing-press will be rolled up as the chief battering-ram. Then there will be a long list of aroused pulpits, which shall be assailing fortresses, and God's red-hot truth shall be the flying ammunition of the contest; and the sappers and the miners will lay the train under these foundations of sin, and at just the right time God, who leads on the fray, will cry, "Down with the gates!" and the explosion beneath will be answered by all the trumpets of God on high celebrating universal victory. But there may be in this house one wanderer that would like to have a kind word calling homeward, and I cannot sit down until I have uttered that word. I have told you that society has no mercy. Did I hint, at an earlier point in this subject, that God will have mercy upon any wanderer who would like to come back to the heart of infinite love?

A cold Christmas night in a farm-house. Father comes in from the barn, knocks the snow from his shoes, and sits down by the fire. The mother sits at the stand knitting. She says to him: "Do you remember it is anniversary to-night?" The father is angered. He never wants any allusion to the fact that one had gone away, and the mere suggestion that it was the anniversary of that sad event made him quite rough, although the tears ran down his cheeks. The old house-dog, that had played with the wanderer when she was a child, came up and put his head on the old man's knee, but he roughly repulsed the dog. He wants nothing to remind him of the anniversary day. The following incident was told me. It was a cold winter night in a city church. It is Christmas night. They have been decorating the sanctuary. A lost wanderer of the street, with thin shawl about her, attracted by the warmth and light, comes in and sits near the door. The minister of religion is preaching of Him who was wounded for our transgressions, and bruised for our iniquities, and the poor soul by the door said: "Why, that must mean me; 'mercy for the chief of sinners; bruised for our iniquities; wounded for our transgressions.'" The music that night in the sanctuary brought back the old hymn which she used to sing when with father and mother she worshiped God in the village church. The service over, the minister went down the aisle. She said to him: "Were those words for me? 'Wounded for our transgressions.' Was that for me?" The man of God understood her not. He knew not how to comfort a shipwrecked soul, and he passed on and he passed out. The poor wanderer followed into the street. "What are you doing here, Meg?" said the police. "What are you doing here to-night?" "Oh!" she replied, "I was in to warm myself;" and then the rattling cough came, and she held to the railing until the paroxysm was over. She passed on down the street, falling from exhaustion; recovering herself again, until after a while she reached the outskirts of the city and passed on into the country road. It seemed so familiar, she kept on the road, and she saw in the distance a light in the window. Ah! that light had been gleaming there every night since she went away. On that country road she passed until she came to the garden gate. She opened it and passed up the path where she played in childhood. She came to the steps and looked in at the fire on the hearth. Then she put her fingers to the latch. Oh! if that door had been locked she would have perished on the threshold, for she was near to death. But that door had not been locked since the time she went away. She pushed open the door. She went in and laid down on the hearth by the fire. The old house-dog growled as he saw her enter, but there was something in the voice he recognized, and he frisked about her until he almost pushed her down in his joy. In the morning the mother came down, and she saw a bundle of rags on the hearth; but when the face was uplifted, she knew it, and it was no more old Meg of the street. Throwing her arms around the returned prodigal, she cried, "Oh! Maggie." The child threw her arms around her mother's neck, and said: "Oh! Mother," and while they were embraced a rugged form towered above them. It was the father. The severity all gone out of his face, he stooped and took her up tenderly and carried her to mother's room, and laid her down on mother's bed, for she was dying. Then the lost one, looking up into her mother's face, said: "'Wounded for our transgressions and bruised for our iniquities!" Mother, do you think that means me?" "Oh, yes, my darling," said the mother, "if mother is so glad to get you back, don't you think God is glad to get you back?" And there she lay dying, and all her dreams and all her prayers were filled with the words, "Wounded for our transgressions, bruised for our iniquities," until just before the moment of her departure, her face lighted up, showing the pardon of God had dropped upon her soul. And there she slept away on the bosom of a pardoning Jesus. So the Lord took back one whom the world rejected.

CHAPTER IV.

WHOM I SAW AND WHOM I MISSED.

"And the vale of Siddim was full of slime-pits."—Genesis xiv: 1..

About six months ago, a gentleman in Augusta, Georgia, wrote me asking me to preach from this text, and the time has come for the subject. The neck of an army had been broken by falling into these half-hidden slime-pits. How deep they were, or how vile, or how hard to get out of, we are not told; but the whole scene is so far distant in the past that we have not half as much interest in this statement of the text as we have in the announcement that our American cities are full of slime-pits, and tens of thousands of people are falling in them night by night. Recently, in the name of God, I explored some of these slime-pits. Why did I do so? In April last, seated in the editorial rooms of one of the chief daily newspapers of New York, the editor said to me: "Mr. Talmage, you clergymen are at great disadvantage when you come to battle iniquity, for you don't know what you are talking about, and we laymen are aware of the fact that you don't know of what you are talking; now, if you would like to make a personal investigation, I will see that you shall get the highest official escort." I thanked him, accepted the invitation, and told him that this autumn I would begin the tour. The fact was that I had for a long time wanted to say some words of warning and invitation to the young men of this country, and I felt if my course of sermons was preceded by a tour of this sort I should not only be better acquainted with the subject, but I should have the whole country for an audience; and it has been a deliberate plan of my ministry, whenever I am going to try to do anything especial for God, or humanity, or the church, to do it in such a way that the devil will always advertise it free gratis for nothing! That was the reason I gave two weeks' previous notice of my pulpit intentions. The result has been satisfactory.

Standing within those purlieus of death, under the command of the police and in their company, I was as much surprised at the people whom I missed as at the people whom I saw. I saw bankers there, and brokers there, and merchants there, and men of all classes and occupations who have leisure, there; but there was one class of persons that I missed. I looked for them all up and down the galleries, and amid the illumined gardens, and all up and down the staircases of death. I saw not one of them. I mean the hard-working classes, the laboring classes, of our great cities. You tell me they could not afford to go there. They could. Entrance, twenty-five cents. They could have gone there if they had a mind to; but the simple fact is that hard work is a friend to good morals. The men who toil from early morn until late at night when they go home are tired out, and want to sit down and rest, or to saunter out with their families along the street, or to pass into some quiet place of amusement where they will not be ashamed to take wife or daughter. The busy populations of these cities are the moral populations. I observed on the night of our exploration that the places of dissipation are chiefly supported by the men who go to business at 9 and 10 o'clock in the morning and get through at 3 and 4 in the afternoon. They have plenty of time to go to destruction in and plenty of money to buy a through ticket on the Grand Trunk Railroad to perdition, stopping at no depot until they get to the eternal smash-up! Those are the fortunate and divinely-blessed young men who have to breakfast early and take supper late, and have the entire interregnum filled up with work that blisters the hands, and makes the legs ache and the brain weary. There is no chance for the morals of that young man who has plenty of money and no occupation. You may go from Central Park to the Battery, or you may go from Fulton Street Ferry, Brooklyn, out to South Bushwick, or out to Hunter's Point, or out to Gowanus, and you will not find one young man of that kind who has not already achieved his ruin, or who is not on the way thereto at the rate of sixty miles the hour. Those are not the favored and divinely-blessed young men who come and go as they will, and who have their pocket-case full of the best cigars, and who dine at Delmonico's, and who dress in the tip-top of fashion, their garments a little tighter or looser or broader striped than others, their mustaches twisted with stiffer cosmetic, and their hair redolent with costly pomatum, and have their hat set farthest over on the right ear, and who have boots fitting the foot with exquisite torture, and who have handkerchief soaked with musk, and patchouli, and white rose, and new-mown hay, and "balm of a thousand flowers;" but those are the fortunate young men who have to work hard for a living. Give a young man plenty of wines, and plenty of cigars, and plenty of fine horses, and Satan has no anxiety about that man's coming out at his place. He ceases to watch him, only giving directions about his reception when he shall arrive at the end of the journey. If, on the night of our exploration, I had called the roll of all the laboring men of these cities, I would have received no answer, for the simple reason they were not there to answer. I was not more surprised at the people whom I saw there than I was surprised at the people whom I missed. Oh! man, if you have an occupation by which you are wearied every night of your life, thank God, for it is the mightiest preservative against evil.

But by that time the clock of old Trinity Church was striking one, two, three, four, five, six, seven, eight, nine, ten, eleven, twelve—midnight! And with the police and two elders of my church we sat down at the table in the galleries and looked off upon the vortex of death. The music in full blast; the dance in wildest whirl; the wine foaming to the lip of the glass. Midnight on earth is midnoon in hell. All the demons of the pit were at that moment holding high carnival. The blue calcium light suggested the burning brimstone of the pit. Seated there, at that hour, in that awful place, you ask me, as I have frequently been asked, "What were the emotions that went through your heart?" And I shall give the rest of my morning's sermon to telling you how I felt.

First of all, as at no death-bed or railroad disaster did I feel an overwhelming sense of pity. Why were we there as Christian explorers, while those lost souls were there as participators? If they had enjoyed the same healthful and Christian surroundings which we have had all our days, and we had been thrown amid the contaminations which have destroyed them, the case would have been the reverse, and they would have been the spectators and we the actors in that awful tragedy of the damned. As I sat there I could not keep back the tears—tears of gratitude to God for his protecting grace—tears of compassion for those who had fallen so low. The difference in moral navigation had been the difference in the way the wind blew. The wind of temptation drove them on the rocks. The wind of God's mercy drove us out on a fair sea. There are men and women so merciless in their criticism of the fallen that you might think that God had made them in an especial mold, and that they have no capacity for evil, and yet if they had been subjected to the same allurements, instead of stopping at the up-town haunts of iniquity, they would at this hour have been wallowing amid the horrors of Arch Block, or shrieking with delirium tremens in the cell of a police station. Instead of boasting over your purity and your integrity and your sobriety, you had better be thanking God for his grace, lest some time the Lord should let you loose and you find out how much better you are than others naturally. I will take the best-tempered man in this house, the most honest man in this city, and I will venture the opinion in regard to him that, surround him with all the adequate circumstances of temptation, and the Lord let him loose, he would become a thief, a gambler, a sot, a rake, a wharf-rat. Instead of boasting over our superiority, and over the fact that there is no capacity in us of evil, I would rather have for my epitaph that one word which Duncan Matthewson, the Scotch evangelist, ordered chiseled on his tombstone, the name, and the one word, "Kept."

Again: Seated in that gallery of death, and looking out on that maelstrom of iniquity, I thought to myself, "There! that young man was once the pride of the city home. Paternal care watched him; maternal love bent over him; sisterly affection surrounded him. He was once taken to the altar and consecrated in the name of the Father, and of the Son, and of the Holy Ghost; but he went away. This very moment," I thought to myself, "there are hearts aching for that young man's return. Father and mother are sitting up for him." You say, "He has a night-key, and he can get in without their help. Why do not those parents go sound to sleep?" What! Is there any sleep for parents who suspect a son is drifting up and down amid the dissipations of a great city? They may weep, they may pray, they may wring their hands, but sleep they cannot. Ah! they have done and suffered too much for that boy to give him up now. They turn up the light and look at the photograph of him when he was young and untempted. They stand at the window to see if he is coming up the street. They hear the watchman's rattle, but no sound of returning boy. I felt that night as if I could put my hand on the shoulder of that young man, and, with a voice that would sound all through those temples of sin, say to him, "Go home, young man; your father is waiting for you. Your mother is waiting for you. God is waiting for you. All heaven is waiting for you. Go home! By the tears wept over your waywardness, by the prayers offered for your salvation, by the midnight watching over you when you had scarlet fever and diphtheria, by the blood of the Son of God, by the judgment day when you must give answer for what you have been doing here to-night, go home!" But I did not say this, lest it interfere with my work, and I waited to get on this platform, where, perhaps, instead of saving one young man, God helping me, I might save a thousand young men; and the cry of alarm which I suppressed that night, I let loose to-day in the hearing of this people.

Seated in that gallery of death, and looking off upon the destruction, I bethought myself also, "These are the fragments of broken homes." A home is a complete thing, and if one member of it wander off, then the home is broken. And sitting there, I said: "Here they are, broken family altars, broken wedding-rings, broken vows, broken anticipations, broken hearts." And, as I looked off, the dance became wilder and more unrestrained, until it seemed as if the floor broke through and the revelers were plunged into a depth from which they may never rise, and all these broken families came around the brink and seemed to cry out: "Come back, father! Come back, mother! Come back, my son! Come back, my daughter! Come back, my sister!" But no voices returned, and the sound of the feet of the dancers grew fainter and fainter, and stopped, and there was thick darkness. And I said, "What does all this mean?" And there came up a great hiss of whispering voices, saying, "This is the second death!"

But seated there that night, looking off upon that scene of death, I bethought myself also, "This is only a miserable copy of European dissipations." In London they have what they call the Argyle, the Cremorne, the Strand, the beer-gardens, and a thousand places of infamy, and it seems to be the ambition of bad people in this country to copy those foreign dissipations. Toadyism when it bows to foreign pretense and to foreign equipage and to foreign title is despicable; but toadyism is more despicable when it bows to foreign vice. Why, you might as well steal the pillow-case of a small-pox hospital, or the shovels of a scavenger's cart, or the coffin of a leper, as to make theft of these foreign plagues. If you want to destroy the people, have some originality of destruction; have an American trap to catch the bodies and souls of men, instead of infringing on the patented inventions of European iniquity.

Seated there that night, I also felt that if the good people of our cities knew what was going on in these haunts of iniquity, they would endure it no longer.

The foundations of city life are rotten with iniquity, and if the foundations give way the whole structure must crumble. If iniquity progresses in the next one hundred years in the same ratio that it has progressed in the century now closed, there will not be a vestige of moral or religious influence left. It is only a question of subtraction and addition. If the people knew how the virus is spreading they would stop it. I think the time has come for action. I wish that the next Mayor of New York whether he be Augustus Schell or Edward Cooper, may rise up to the height of this position. Revolution is what we want, and that revolution would begin to-morrow if the moral and Christian people of our cities knew of the fires that slumber beneath them. Once in a while a glorious city missionary or reformer like Mr. Brace or Mr. Van Meter tells to a well-dressed audience in church the troubles that lie under our roaring metropolis, and the conventional church-goer gives his five dollars for bread, or gives his fifty dollars to help support a ragged school, and then goes home feeling that the work is done. Oh! my friends, the work will not be accomplished until by the force of public opinion the officers of the law shall be compelled to execute the law. We are told that the twenty-five hundred police of New York cannot put down the five or six hundred dens of infamy, to say nothing of the gambling-houses and the unlicensed grog-shops. I reply, swear me in as a special police and give me two hundred police for two nights, and I would break up all the leading haunts of iniquity in these two cities, and arrest all their leaders and send such consternation in the smaller places that they would shut up of themselves! I do not think I should be afraid of law-suits for damages for false imprisonment. What we want in these cities is a Stonewall Jackson's raid through all the places of iniquity. I was persuaded by what I saw on that night of my exploration that the keepers of all these haunts of iniquity are as afraid as they are of death of the police star, and the police club, and the police revolver. Hence, I declare that the existence of these abominations are to be charged either to police cowardice or to police complicity.

At the close of our journey that night, we got in the carriage, and we came out on Broadway, and as we came down the street everything seemed silent save the clattering hoofs and the wheels of our own conveyance. Looking down the long line of gaslights, the pavement seemed very solitary. The great sea of metropolitan life had ebbed, leaving a dry beach! New York asleep! No! no! Burglary wide awake. Libertinism wide awake. Murder wide awake. Ten thousand city iniquities wide awake. The click of the decanters in the worst hours of the debauch. The harvest of death full. Eternal woe the reaper.

What is that? Trinity clock striking, one--two. "Good night," said the officers of the law, and I responded "good night," for they had been very kind, and very generous and very helpful to us. "Good night." And yet, was there ever an adjective more misapplied? Good night! Why, there was no expletive enough scarred and blasted to describe that night. Black night. Forsaken night. Night of man's wickedness and woman's overthrow. Night of awful neglect on the part of those who might help but do not. For many of those whom we had been watching, everlasting night. No hope. No rescue. No God. Black night of darkness forever. As far off as hell is from heaven was that night distant from being a good night. Oh, my friends, what are you going to do in this matter? Punish the people? That is not my theory. Prevent the people, warn the people, hinder the people before they go down. The first philanthropist this country ever knew was Edward Livingston, and he wrote these remarkable words in 1833:

"As prevention in the diseases of the body is less painful, less expensive, and more efficacious than the most skillful cure, so in the moral maladies of society, to arrest the vicious before the profligacy assumes the shape of crime, to take away from the poor the cause or pretense of relieving themselves by fraud or theft, to reform them by education, and make their own industry contribute to their support, although difficult and expensive, will be found more effectual inthe suppression of offenses, and more economical, than the best organized system of punishment."

Next Sabbath morning I shall tell you of my second night of exploration. I have only opened the door of this great subject with which I hope to stir the cities. I have begun, and, God helping me, I will go through. Whoever else may be crowded or kept standing, or kept outside the doors, I charge the trustees and the ushers of this church that they give full elbow-room to all these journalists, since each one is another church five times, or ten times, or twenty times larger than this august assemblage, and it is by the printing-press that the Gospel of the Son of God is to be yet preached to all the world. May the blessing of the Lord God come down upon all the editors, and all the reporters, and all the compositors, and all the proof-readers, and all the type-setters!

But, my friends, before the iniquities of our cities are closed, my tongue may be silent in death, and many who are here this morning may have gone so far in sin they cannot get back. You have sometimes been walking on the banks of a river, and you have seen a man struggling in the water, and you have thrown off your coat and leaped in for the rescue. So this morning I throw off the robe of pulpit conventionality, and I plunge in for your drowning soul. I have no cross words for you. I have only cross words for those who would destroy you. I am glad God has not put in my hand any one of the thunderbolts of His power, lest I might be tempted to hurl it at those who are plotting your ruin. I do not give you the tip end of the long fingers of the left hand, but I take your hand, hot with the fever of indulgences and trembling with last night's debauch, into both my hands, and give the heartiest grip of invitation and welcome. "Oh," you say, "you would not shake hands with me if you met me." I would. Try me at the foot of this platform and see if I will not. I have sometimes said that I would like to die with my hand in the hand of my family and my kindred; but I revoke that wish this morning and say I would like to die with my hand in the hand of a returning sinner, when, with God's help, I am trying to pull him up into the glorious liberty of the Gospel. I would like that to be my last work on earth. Oh! my brother, come back! Do you know that God made Richard Baxters and John Bunyans and Robert Newtons out of such as you are? Come back! and wash in the deep fountain of a Savior's mercy. I do not give you a cup, or a chalice, or a pitcher with a limited supply to effect your ablutions. I point you to the five oceans of God's mercy. Oh! that the Atlantic and Pacific surges of divine forgiveness might roll over your soul. I do not say to you, as we said to the officers of the law when we left them on Broadway, "Good night." Oh, no. But, as the glorious sun of God's forgiveness rides on toward the mid heavens, ready to submerge you in warmth and light and love, I bid you good morning! Morning of peace for all your troubles. Morning of liberation for all your incarcerations. Morning of resurrection for your soul buried in sin. Good morning! Morning for the resuscitated household that has been waiting for your return. Morning for the cradle and the crib already disgraced with being that of a drunkard's child. Morning for the daughter that has trudged off to hard work because you did not take care of home. Morning for the wife who at forty or fifty years has the wrinkled face, and the stooped shoulder, and the white hair. Morning for one. Morning for all. Good morning! In God's name, good morning.

In our last dreadful war the Federals and the Confederates were encamped on opposite sides of the Rappahannock, and one morning the brass band of the Northern troops played the national air, and all the Northern troops cheered and cheered. Then on the opposite side of the Rappahannock the brass band of the Confederates played "My Maryland" and "Dixie," and then all the Southern troops cheered and cheered. But after awhile one of the bands struck up "Home, Sweet Home," and the band on the opposite side of the river took up the strain, and when the tune was done the Confederates and the Federals all together united, as the tears rolled down their cheeks, in one great huzza! huzza! Well, my friends, heaven comes very near to-day. It is only a stream that divides us—the narrow stream of death—and the voices there and the voices here seem to commingle, and we join trumpets, and hosannahs, and hallelujahs, and the chorus of the united song of earth and heaven is, "Home, Sweet Home." Home of bright domestic circle on earth. Home of forgiveness in the great heart of God. Home of eternal rest in heaven. Home! Home! Home!

CHAPTER V.

UNDER THE POLICE LANTERN.

The destruction of the poor is their poverty.—Proverbs x: 15.

On an island nine miles long by two and a half wide stands the largest city on this continent—a city mightiest for virtue and for vice. Before I get through with this series of Sabbath morning discourses, I shall show you the midnoon of its magnificent progress and philanthropy, as well as the midnight of its crime and sin. Twice in every twenty-four hours our City Hall and old Trinity clocks strike twelve—once while business and art are in full blast, and once while iniquity is doing its uttermost. Both stories must be told. It is pleasanter to put on a plaster than to thrust in a probe; but it is absurd to propose remedies for disease until we have taken a diagnosis of that disease. The patient may squirm and cringe, and fight back, and resist; but the surgeon must go on. Before I get through with these Sabbath morning sermons, I shall make you all smile at the beautiful things I will say about the grandeur and beneficence of this cluster of cities; but my work now is excavation and exposure. I have as much amusement as any man of my profession can afford to indulge in at any one time, in seeing some of the clerical "reformers" of this day mount their war-charger, dig in their spurs, and with glittering lance dash down upon the iniquities of cities that have been three or four thousand years dead. These men will corner an old sinner of twenty or thirty centuries ago, and scalp him, and hang him, and cut him to pieces, and then say: "Oh! what great things have been done." With amazing prowess, they throw sulphur at Sodom, and fire at Gomorrah, and worms at Herod, and pitch Jezebel over the wall, but wipe off their gold spectacles, and put on their best kid gloves, and unroll their morocco-covered sermon, and look bashful when they begin to speak about the sins of our day, as though it were a shame even to mention them. The hypocrites! They are afraid of the libertines and the men who drink too much, in their churches, and those who grind the face of the poor. Better, I say, clear out all our audiences from pulpit to storm-door, until no one is left but the sexton, and he staying merely to lock up, than to have the pulpit afraid of the pew. The time has come when the living Judases and Herods and Jezebels are to be arraigned. There is one thing I like about a big church: a dozen people may get mad about the truth and go off, and you don't know they are gone until about the next year. The cities standing on the ground are the cities to be reformed, and not the Herculaneums buried under volcanic ashes, or the cities of the plain fifty feet under the Dead Sea.

I unroll the scroll of new revelations. With city missionary, and the police of New York and Brooklyn, I have seen some things that I have not yet stated in this series of discourses on the night side of city life. The night of which I speak now is darker than any other. No glittering chandelier, no blazing mirror adorns it. It is the long, deep exhaustive night of city pauperism. "We won't want a carriage to-night," said the detectives. "A carriage would hinder us in our work; a carriage going through the streets where we are going would only bring out the people to see what was the matter." So on foot we went up the dark lanes of poverty Everything revolting to eye, and ear, and nostril. Population unwashed, uncombed. Rooms unventilated. Three midnights overlapping each other—midnight of the natural world, midnight of crime, midnight of pauperism. Stairs oozing with filth. The inmates, nine-tenths of the journey to their final doom, traveled. They started in some unhappy home of the city or of the country. They plunged into the shambles of death within ten minutes' walk of the Fifth Avenue Hotel, New York, and then came on gradually down until they have arrived at the Fourth Ward. When they move out of the Fourth Ward they will move into Bellevue Hospital; when they move out of Bellevue Hospital they will move to Blackwell's Island; when they move from Blackwell's Island they will move to the Potter's Field; when they move from the Potter's Field they will move into hell! Bellevue Hospital and Blackwell's Island take care of 18,000 patients in one year. As we passed on, the rain pattering on the street and dripping around the doorways made the night more dismal. I said, "Now let the police go ahead," and they flashed their light, and there were fourteen persons trying to sleep, or sleeping, in one room. Some on a bundle of straw; more with nothing under them and nothing over them. "Oh!" you say, "this is exceptional." It is not. Thousands lodge in that way. One hundred and seventy thousand families living in tenement houses, in more or less inconvenience, more or less squalor. Half a million people in New York city—five hundred thousand people living in tenement-houses; multitudes of these people dying by inches. Of the twenty-four thousand that die yearly in New York fourteen thousand die in tenement-houses. No lungs that God ever made could for a long while stand the atmosphere we breathed for a little while. In the Fourth

Ward, 17,000 people within the space of thirty acres. You say, "Why not clear them out? Why not, as at Liverpool, where 20,000 of these people were cleared out of the city, and the city saved from a moral pestilence, and the people themselves from being victimized?" There will be no reformation for these cities until the tenement-house system is entirely broken up. The city authorities will have to buy farms, and will have to put these people on those farms, and compel them to work. By the strong arm of the law, by the police lantern conjoined with Christian charity, these places must be exposed and must be uprooted. Those places in London which have become historical for crowded populations—St. Giles, Whitechapel, Holborn, the Strand—have their match at last in the Sixth Ward, Eleventh Ward, Fourteenth Ward, Seventeenth Ward of New York. No purification for our cities until each family shall have something of the privacy and seclusion of a home circle. As long as they herd like beasts, they will be beasts.

Hark! What is that heavy thud on the wet pavement? Why, that is a drunkard who has fallen, his head striking against the street—striking very hard. The police try to lift him up. Ring the bell for the city ambulance. No. Only an outcast, only a tatterdemalion—a heap of sores and rags. But look again. Perhaps he has some marks of manhood on his face; perhaps he may have been made in the image of God; perhaps he has a soul which will live after the dripping heavens of this dismal night have been rolled together as a scroll; perhaps he may have been died for, by a king; perhaps he may yet be a conqueror charioted in the splendors of heavenly welcome. But we must pass on. We cross the street, and, the rain beating in his face, lies a man entirely unconscious. I wonder where he came from. I wonder if any one is waiting for him. I wonder if he was ever rocked in a Christian cradle. I wonder if that gashed and bloated forehead was ever kissed by a fond mother's lips. I wonder if he is stranded for eternity. But we cannot stop. We passed on down, the air loaded with blasphemies and obscenities, until I heard something that astounded me more than all. I said, "What is that?" It was a loud, enthusiastic Christian song, rolling out on the stormy air. I went up to the window and looked in. There was a room filled with all sorts of people, some standing, some kneeling, some sitting, some singing, some praying, some shaking hands as if to give encouragement, some wringing their hands as though over a wasted life. What was this? Oh! it was Jerry McAuley's glorious Christian mission. There he stood, himself snatched from death, snatching others from death. That scene paid for all the nausea and fatigue of the midnight exploration. Our tears fell with the rain—tears of sympathy for a good man's work; tears of gratitude to God that one lifeboat had been launched on that wild sea of sin and death; tears of hope that there might be lifeboats enough to take off all the wrecked, and, that, after a while, the Church of God, rousing from its fastidiousness, might lay hold with both hands of this work, which must be done if our cities are not to go down in darkness and fire and blood.

This cluster of cities have more difficulty than any other cities in all the land. You must understand that within the last twenty-eight years five millions of foreign population have arrived at our port. The most of those who had capital and means passed on to the greater openings at the West. Many however, stayed and have become our best citizens, and best members of our churches; but we know also that, tarrying within our borders, there has been a vast criminal population ready to be manipulated by the demagogue, ready to hatch out all kinds of criminal desperation. The vagrancy and the beggary of our cities, augmented by the very worst populations of London and Edinburg, and Glasgow, and Berlin, and Belfast, and Dublin and Cork. We had enough vagabondage, and enough turpitude in our American cities before this importation of sin was dumped at Castle Garden. Oh! this pauperism, when will it ever be alleviated? How much we saw! How much we could not see! How much none but the eye of Almighty God will ever see! Flash the lantern of the police around to that station-house. There they come up, the poor creatures, tipping their torn hats, saying, "Night's lodging, sir?" And then they are waived away into the dormitories. One hundred and forty thousand such lodgers in the city of New York every year. The atmosphere unbearable. What pathos in the fact that many families turned out of doors because they cannot pay their rent, come in here for shelter, and after struggling for decency, and struggling for a good name, are flung into this loathsome pool. The respectable and the reprobate. Innocent childhood and vicious old age. The Lord's poor and Satan's desperadoes. There is no report of almshouse and missionary that will ever tell the story of New York and Brooklyn pauperism. It will take a larger book, a book with more ponderous lids, a book made of paper other than that of earthly manufacture. The book of God's remembrance! At my basement door we average between fifty and one hundred calls every day for help. Beside that, in my reception room, from 7 o'clock in the morning until 10 o'clock at night, there is a continuous procession of people applying for aid, making a demand which an old-fashioned silken purse, caught at the middle with a ring, the wealth of Vanderbilt in one end and the wealth of William B. Astor in the other end, could not satisfy. Of course, I speak of those men's wealth while they lived. We have more money now than they have since they have their shroud on. But even the shroud and the grave, we find, are to be contested for. Cursed be the midnight jackals of St. Mark's Churchyard! But I must go on with the fact that the story of Brooklyn and New York pauperism needs to be written in ink, black, blue and red—blue for the stripes, red for the blood, black for the infamy. In this cluster of cities 20,000 people supported by the bureau for the outdoor sick; 20,000 people taken care of by the city hospitals; 70,000 provided for by private charity; 80,000 taken care of by reformatory institutions and prisons. Hear it, ye churches, and pour out your benefaction. Hear it, you ministers of religion, and utter words of sympathy for the suffering, and thunders of indignation against the cause of all this wretchedness. Hear it, mayoralties and judicial bench, and constabularies. Unless we wake up, the Lord will scourge us as the yellow fever never scourged New Orleans, as the plague never smote London, as the earthquake never shook Carraccas, as the fire never overwhelmed Sodom. I wish I could throw a bombshell of arousal into every city hall, meeting-house and cathedral on the continent. The factories at Fall River and at Lowell sometimes stop for lack of demand, and for lack of workmen, but this million-roomed factory of sin and death never stops, never slackens a band, never arrests a spindle. The great wheel of that factory keeps on turning, not by such floods as those of the Merrimac or the Connecticut, but crimson floods rushing forth from the groggeries, and the wine-cellars, and the drinking saloons of the land, and the faster the floods rush the faster the wheel turns; and the band of that wheel is woven from broken heart-strings, and every time the wheel turns, from the mouth of the mill come forth blasted estates, squalor, vagrancy, crime, sin, woe—individual woe, municipal woe, national woe—and the creaking and the rumbling of the wheels are the shrieks and the groans of men and women lost for two worlds, and the cry is, "Bring on more fortunes, more homes, more States, more cities, to make up the awful grist of this stupendous mill." "Oh," you say, "the wretchedness and the sin of the city will go out from lack of material after awhile." No, it will not. The police lantern flashes in another direction. Here come 15,000 shoeless, hatless, homeless children of the street, in this cluster of cities. They are the reserve corps of this great army of wretchedness and crime that are dropping down into the Morgue, the East river, the Potter's Field, the prison. A philanthropist has estimated that if these children were placed in a great procession, double-file, three feet apart, they would make a procession eleven miles long. Oh! what a pale, coughing, hunger-bitten, sin-cursed, opthalmic throng—the tigers, the adders, the scorpions ready to bite and sting society, which they take to be their natural enemy. Howard Mission has saved many. Children's Aid Society has saved many. Industrial Schools have saved many. One of these societies transported 30,000 children from the streets of our cities, to farms at the West, by a stratagem of charity, turning them from vagrancy into useful citizenship, and out of 21,000 children thus transported from the cities to farms only twelve turned out badly. But still the reserve corps of sin and wretchedness marches on. There is the regiment of boot-blacks. They seem jolly, but they have more sorrow than many an old man has had. All kinds of temptation. Working on, making two or three dollars a week. At fifteen years of age sixty years old in sin. Pitching pennies at the street corners. Smoking fragments of castaway cigars. Tempted by the gamblers. Destroyed by the top gallery in the low play house. Blacking shoes their regular business. Between times blackening their morals. "Shine your boots, sir?" they call out with merry voices, but there is a tremor in their accentuation. Who cares for them? You put your foot thoughtlessly on their stand, and you whistled or smoked, when God knows you might have given them one kind word. They never had one. Whoever prayed for a bootblack? Who, finding the wind blowing under the short jacket, or reddening his bare neck, ever asked him to warm? Who, when he is wronged out of his ter cents, demands justice for him? God have mercy or the bootblacks. The newsboys, another regiment—the smartest boys in all the city. At work at four o'clock in the morning. At half-past three, by unnatural vigilance, awake themselves, or pulled at by rough hands. In the dawn of the day standing before the folding-rooms of the great newspapers, taking the wet, damp sheets over their arms, and against their chests already shivering with the cold. Around the bleak ferries, and up and down the streets on the cold days, singing as merrily as though it were a Christmas carol; making half a cent on each paper, some of them working fourteen hours for fifty cents! Nine thousand of these newsboys applied for aid at the Newsboys' Lodging-house on Park place, New York, in one year. About one thousand of them laid up in the savings bank connected with that institution, a little more than $3,000. But still this great army marches on, hungry, cold, sick, toward an early grave, or a quick prison. I tell you there is nothing that so moves my compassion as on a cold winter morning to see one of these newsboys, a fourth clad, newspapers on his arm that he cannot seem to sell, face or hands bleeding from a fall, or rubbing his knee to relieve it from having been hit on the side of a car, as some "gentleman," with furs around his neck and gauntlets lined with lamb's wool, shoved him off, saying: "You miserable rat!" Yet hawking the papers through the streets, papers full of railroad accidents and factory explosions, and steamers foundering at sea in the last storm, yet saying nothing, and that which is to him worse than all the other calamities and all the other disasters, the calamity that he was ever born at all. Flash the police lantern around, and let us see these poor lads cuddled up under the stairway. Look at them! Now for a little while they are unconscious of all their pains and aches, and of the storm and darkness, once in awhile struggling in their dreams as though some one were trying to take the papers away from them. Standing there I wondered if it would be right to wish that they might never wake up. God pity them! There are other regiments in this reserve corps—regiments of rag-pickers, regiments of match-sellers, regiments of juvenile vagrants. Oh! if these lads are not saved, what is to become of our cities?

But I said to the detective, "I have had enough of this to-night; let us go." But by that time I had lost the points of the compass, for we had gone down stairways and up stairways, and wandered down through this street and that street, and all I knew was that I was bounded on the north by want, and on the south by squalor, and on the east by crime, and on the west by despair. The fact was that everything had opened before us; for these detectives pretended to be searching for a thief, and they took me along as the man who had lost the property!

The stratagem was theirs, not mine. But I thought coming home that rainy night, I wished I could make pass before my congregation, as in a panorama, all that scene of suffering, that I might stir their pity and arouse their beneficence, and make them the everlasting friends of city evangelization. "Why," you say, "I had no idea things were so bad. Why, I get in my carriage at Forty-fifth street and I ride clear down to my banking-house in Wall street, and I don't see anything." No, you do not want to see! The King and the Parliament of England did not know that there were thirty-six barrels of gunpowder rolled into the vaults under the Parliament House. They did not know Guy Fawkes had his touchwood and matches all ready—ready to dash the Government of England into atoms. The conspiracy was revealed, however. I tell you I have explored the vaults of city life, and I am here this morning to tell you that there are deathful and explosive influences under all our cities, ready to destroy us with a great moral convulsion. Some men say: "I don't see anything of this, and I am not interested in it." You ought to be. You remind me of a man who has been shipwrecked with a thousand others. He happens to get up on the shore, and the others are all down in the surf. He goes up in a fisherman's cabin, and sits down to warm himself. The fisherman says: "Oh! this won't do. Come out and help me to get these others out of the surf." "Oh, no!" says the man; "it's my business now to warm myself." "But," says the fisherman, "these men are dying; are you not going to give them help?" "Oh, no! I've got ashore myself, and I must warm myself!" That is what people are doing in the church to-day. A great multitude are out in the surf of sin and death, going down forever; but men sit by the fire of the church, warming their Christian graces, warming their faith, warming their hope for heaven, and I say, "Come out, and work to-day for Christ." "Oh, no," they say; "my sublime duty is to warm myself!" Such men as that will not come within ten thousand miles of heaven! Help foreign missions. Those of my own blood are toiling in foreign lands with Christ's Word. Send a million dollars for the salvation of the heathen—that is right—but look after the heathen also around the mouths of the Hudson and East rivers. Send missionaries if you will to Borioboola-gha, but send missionaries also through Houston street, Mercer street, Greene street, Navy street, Fulton street, and all around about Brooklyn Atlantic Docks. If you will, send quilted coverlets to Central Africa to keep the natives warm in summer-time, and send ice-cream freezers to Greenland, but do have a little common sense and practical charity, and help these cities here that want hats, want clothes, want shoes, want fire, want medicines, want instruction, want the Gospel, want Christ.

I must adjourn to another Sabbath morning much of what I have to say in regard to this city midnight exploration, and also the proposing of remedies; for I am not the man to stand here Sabbath by Sabbath talking of ills when I have no panacea. There is an almighty rescue for the city, and in due time I will speak of these things.

You have seen often a magic lantern. You have seen the room darkened, and then the magic lantern throwing a picture on the canvas. Well, this morning I wish I could darken these three great emblazoned windows, and have all the doors darkened, and then I could bring out two magic lanterns—the magic lantern of the home, and the magic lantern of the police. Here is the magic lantern of the home. Look now upon the canvas. Mother putting the little children to bed, trying to hush the frisky and giggling group for the evening prayer; their foreheads against the counterpane, they are trying to say their evening prayer; their tongue is so crooked that none but God and the mother can understand it. Then the children are lifted into bed, and they are covered up to the chin. Then the mother gives them a warm good-night kiss, and leaves them to the guardian angels that spread wings of canopy over the trundle-bed. Midnight lantern of the police. Look now on the canvas. A boy kenneled for the night underneath the stairway in a hall through which the wind sweeps, or lying on the cold ground. He had no parentage. He was pitched into the world by a merciless incognito. He does not go to bed; he has no bed. His cold fingers thrust through his matted hair his only pillow. He did not sup last night; he will not breakfast to-morrow. An outcast; a ragamuffin. He did not say his prayers when he retired; he knows no prayer; he never heard the name of God or Christ, except as something to swear by. The wings over him, not the wings of angels, but the dark, bat-like wings of penury and want. Magic lantern of the home. Look now on the canvas. Family gathered around the argand burner. Father, feet on ottoman, mother sewing a picturesque pattern. Two children pretending to study, but chiefly watching other children who are in unrestrained romp, so many balls of fun and frolic in full bounce from room to room. Background of pictures and upholstery and musical instrument, from which jeweled fingers sweep "Home, Sweet Home." Magic lantern of the police. Look now on the canvas. A group intoxicated and wrangling, cursing God, cursing each other; the past all shame, the future all suffering. Children fleeing from the missile flung by a father's hand.

Fragments of a chair propped against the wall. Fragments of a pitcher standing on the mantle. A pile of refuse food brought in from some kitchen, torn by the human swine plunging into the trough. Magic lantern of the home. Look now upon the canvas. A Christian daughter has just died. Carriages rolling up to the door in sympathy. Flowers in crowns and anchors and harps covering the beautiful casket, the silver plate marked, "aged 18." Funeral services intoned amid the richly-shawled and gold-braceleted. Long procession going out this way to unparalleled Greenwood to the beautiful family plot where the sculptor will raise the monument of burnished Aberdeen with the inscription, 'She is not dead, but sleepeth." Oh! blessed is that home which has a consecrated Christian daughter, whether on earth or in heaven. Magic lantern of the police. Look now on the canvas. A poor waif of the street has just expired. Did she have any doctor? No. Did she have any medicine? No. Did she have any hands to close her eyes and fold her arms in death? No. Are there no garments in the house fit to wrap her in for the tomb? None. Those worn-out shoes will not do for these feet in their last journey. Where are all the good Christians? Oh! some of them are rocking-chaired, in morning gowns, in tears over Bulwer Lytton's account of the last days of Pompeii; they are so sorry for that girl that got petrified! Others of the Christians are in church, kneeling on a soft rug, praying for the forlorn Hottentots! Come, call in the Coroner—call in the Charity Commissioner. The carpenter unrolls the measuring-tape, and decides she will need a box five and a half feet long. Two men lift her into the box, lift the box into the wagon, and it starts for the Potter's Field. The excavation is not large enough for the box, and the men are in a hurry, and one of them gets on the lid and cranches it down to its place in the ground. Stop! Wait for the city missionary until he can come and read a chapter, or say, "Ashes to ashes, dust to dust." "No," say the men of the spade, "we have three or four more cases just like this to bury before night." "Well," I say, "how, then, is the grave to be filled up?" Christ suggests a way. Perhaps it had better be filled up with stones. "Let those who are without sin come and cast a stone at her," until the excavation is filled. Then the wagon rolls off, and I see a form coming slowly across the Potter's Field. He walks very slowly, as his feet hurt. He comes to that grave, and there he stands all day and all night, and I come out and I accost him, and I say, "Who art thou?" And he says, "I am the Christ of Mary Magdalen!" And then I thought that perhaps there might have been a dying prayer, and that there might have been penitential tears, and around that miserable spot at the last there may be more resurrection pomp than when Queen Elizabeth gets out of her mausoleum in Westminster Abbey.

But I must close the two lanterns.

CHAPTER VI.

SATANIC AGITATION.

"The devil is come down unto you, having great wrath, because he knoweth he hath but a short time."—Revelation xii: 12.

Somehow the enemy of all good has found out what will be the hour of his dismissal from this world. He cried out to Christ: "Hast thou come to torment us before *the* time?" It is a healthful symptom that Satan is so active now in all our cities. It is the indication that he is going out of business. From the way that he flies around, he is practically saying: "Give me 500,000 souls; give me New York and Brooklyn; give me Boston and Philadelphia and Cincinnati; give me all the cities, and give them to me quickly, or I will never get them at all." That Satan is in paroxysm of excitement is certain. His establishments are nearly bankrupted. That the powers of darkness are nervous, knowing their time is short, is evident from the fact that, if a man stand in a pulpit speaking against the great iniquities of the day, they all begin to flutter.

A few nights ago, riding up Broadway, I asked the driver to stop at a street-lamp that I might better examine my memorandum (it happened to be in front of a place of amusement), when a man rushed out with great alarm and excitement, and said to the driver, "Is that Talmage you have inside there?" Men write me with commercial handwriting, protesting, evidently because they fear that sometimes in their midnight carousal they may meet a Christian reformer and explorer. I had thought to preach three or four sermons on the night side of city life ; but now that I find that all the powers of darkness are so agitated and alarmed and terrorized, I plant the battery for new assault upon the castles of sin, and shall go on from Sabbath morning to Sabbath morning, saying all I have to say, winding up this subject by several sermons on the glorious daybreak of Christian reform and charity which have made this cluster of cities the best place on earth to live in. Meanwhile, understand that whatever Satanic excitement may be abroad is only in fulfillment of the words of my text: "The devil is come down unto you, having great wrath, because he knoweththat he hath but a short time."

A few nights ago, passing over from Brooklyn by South Ferry, our great metropolis looked like a mountain of picturesqueness and beauty. There were enough stars scattered over the heavens to suggest the street-lamps of that city which hath no need of the sun. The masts of the shipping against the sky brought to us the cosmopolitan feeling, and I said, "All the world is here." The spires of St. Paul's, and St. George's, and of Trinity pointed up through the starlight toward the only rescue for the dying populations of our great cities. Long rows of lamps skirted the city with fire. More than ten thousand gaslights, united with those kindled in towers and in the top stories of establishments which ply great industries in perpetual motion, threw on the sky from horizon to horizon the radiance of a vast illumination. Landing on New York side, the first thing that confronted us was the greatest nuisance and the grandest relief which New York has experienced in the last thirty years, the elevated railway, which, while it has commercial significance, has more moral meaning. Ruin and death to the streets through which it runs, it is the means of moral salvation to the crowded and smothered tenement-houses, which have been slaying their thousands year by year. Was there ever such a disfigurement and sacrification of carpentry and engineering that wrought such a blissful result? The great obstacle to New York morals is the shape of the island. More than nine miles long, in some places it is only a mile and a half wide. While this immense water frontage of twenty miles is grand for commerce, it gives crowded residence to the population, unless, by some rapid mode of transit, they can be whirled to distant homes at night, and whirled back again in the morning. These people must be near their work. Some of them do not like ferriage. Many of them are afraid of water. From the looks of some of their hands and faces, you find it proved that they are afraid of water. Hence they are huddled together in tenement-houses, which are the destruction of all health, all modesty, and the highest style of morals. For the last thirty years New York has been crowded to death. Hence, when on the night of our exploration we saw the rail-train flying through the air, I said to myself, "This is the first practical alleviation of the tenement-house system." People of small means will have an opportunity of getting to the better air and the better morals and the better accomodations of the country. But let not this style of improvement be made at the expense of those whose property is destroyed by the clatter and bang and wheeze of mid-air locomotive. Let cities, like individuals, pay for damages wrought, and for horses frightened out of their harness, and for carriages smashed against the curbstone. New York and Brooklyn and all our great cities need what London has already gained—

underground railroads which shall, without hindrance and without danger and without nuisance, put down our great populations just where they want to be, morning and night.

Passing up through the city, on the left was Castle Garden, now comparatively unattractive; but as we went past, my boyhood memory brought back to me the time when all that region was crowded with the finest equipages of New York and Brooklyn, and Castle Garden was thronged with a great multitude, many of whom had paid $14 for a seat to hear Jenny Lind sing. While God might make a hundred such artists in a year, He makes only one for a century. He who heard her sing would have no right to complain if he never heard any more music until he heard the doxology of the one hundred and forty and four thousand. There was the music of two worlds in her voice. While surrounded by those who almost deified her, she wrote in a private album a verse which it may not be wrong to quote:

In vain I seek for rest
  In all created good;
It leaves me still unblest
  And makes me cry for God.
And sure at rest I cannot be
Until my heart finds rest in Thee.

That was the secret of her music, and never, either day or night, do I pass Castle Garden, but I think of the Swedish cantatrice and the excited and vociferating assemblage, the majority of whom have joined the larger assemblages of the next world.

Passing on up into New York, we left on the right hand, the once fashionable Bowling Green, around which the wealth of New York congregated—the once elegant drawing-rooms, now occupied by steamship companies, where passengers get booked for Glasgow and Liverpool; the inhabitants of those once elegant drawing-rooms long ago booked for a longer voyage. Passing on up, we heard only the clatter of the horses' hoofs until we came to the head of Wall street, and by the two rows of gas-lights, saw that on all that street there was not a foot stirring. And yet there seemed to come up on the night air the cachinnation of those on whose hands the stocks had gone up, and the sighing of jobbers on whose hands the stocks had gone down. The street, only half a mile long, and yet the avenue of fabulous accumulation, and appalling bankruptcy, and wild swindle, and suicide, and catastrophe, and death! While the sough of the wind came up from Wall street toward old Trinity, it seemed to say: "Where is Ketcham? Where is Swartwout? Where is Gay? Where is Fisk? Where is Cornelius Vanderbilt? Where is the Black Friday?" Then the tower of Trinity tolled nine times—three for the bankrupted, three for the suicided, three for the dead! "Hurry up, George," I said, "and get past this place;" for though I do not believe in ghosts, I wanted to get past that forsaken and all-suggestive night-scene of Wall street. Under the flickering gaslight one of active imagination might almost imagine he saw the ghosts of ten thousand fortunes dead and damned. Hastening on up a few blocks, we came where, on the right side, we saw large establishments ablaze from foundation to cap-stone. These were the great printing-houses of the New York dailies. We got out. We went in. We went up from editorial rooms to type-setters' and proof-readers' loft. These are the foundries where the great thunder-bolts of public opinion are forged. How the pens scratched! How the types clicked! How the scissors cut! How the wheels rushed, all the world's news rolling over the cylinder like Niagara at Table Rock. Great torrents of opinion, of crimes, of accidents, of destroyed reputations, of avenged character. Who can estimate the mightiness for good or evil of a daily newspaper? Fingers of steel picking off the end of telegraphic wire, facts of religion and philosophy and science, and information from the four winds of heaven! In 1850 the Associated Press began to pay $200,000 a year for news. Some of the individual sheets paying $50,000 extra for dispatches. Some of them, independent of the Associated Press, with a wire rake gathering up sheaves of news from all the great harvest fields of the world. It is high time that good men understood that the printing press is the mightiest engine of all the centuries. The high-water mark of the printer's type-case shows the ebb or flow of the great oceanic tides of civilization or Christianity. Just think of it! In 1835 all the daily newspapers of New York issued but 10,000 copies. Now there are 500,000, and taking the ordinary calculation that five people read a newspaper, two million, five hundred thousand people reading the daily newspapers of New York! I once could not understand how the Bible statement could be true when it says that "nations shall be born in a day." I can understand it now. Get the telegraph operators and the editors converted, and in twenty-four hours the whole earth will hear the salvation call. Nothing more impressed me in the night exploration than the power of the press. But it is carried on with oh! what aching eyes, and what exhaustion of health. I did not find more than one man out of ten who had anything like brawny health in the great newspaper establishments of New York. The malodor of the ink, however complete the ventilation; the necessity of toiling at hours when God has drawn the curtain of the night for natural sleep; the pressure of daily publication whatever breaks down; the temptation to intoxicating stimulants in order to keep the nervous energy up, a temptation which only the strongest can resist—all these make newspaper life something to be sympathized with. Do not begrudge the three or five cents you give for the newspaper. You buy not only intelligence with that, but you help pay for sleepless nights, and smarting eyeballs, and racked brain, and early sepulchre.

Coming out of these establishments, my mind full of the bewildering activities of the place, I stopped on the street and I said, "Now drive up Broadway, and turn down Chambers street to the left, and let us see what New York will be twenty years from now." The probability is that those who are criminal will stay criminal; the vast majority of those who are libertines will remain libertines; the vast majority of those who are thieves will stay thieves; the vast majority of those who are drunkards will stay drunkards. "What," say you, "no hope for the cities?" Ah! my heart was never so full of high and exhilarant hope as now. We turned down Chambers street until we came to the sign "Newsboys' Lodging-house," and we went in. Now, if there is anything I like it is boys. Not those brought up by registers, with the house heated by furnaces, and lads manipulated by some over-indulgent aunt, until their hair has bean curled until they have got to be girls; but I mean genuine boys, such as God makes, with extra romp and hilarity, so that after they have been pounded by the world they shall have some exuberance left. Boys, genuine boys, who cannot keep quiet five minutes. Boys who can skate, and swim, and rove, and fly kites, and strike balls, and defend sickly playmates when they are imposed on, and get hungry in half an hour after they have dined, and who keep things stirred up and lively. Matthew Arnold's boys.

We entered the Newsboys' Lodging-house, and there we found them. I knew them right away, and they knew me, by a sort of instinct of friendliness. Their coats off; for, although outside it was biting cold, inside the room Christian charity had flooded everything with glorious summer. Over the doorway were written the words: "No boys that have homes can stop here." "What," I said, "can it be possible that all these bright and happy lads have been swept up from the street?" First, they are plunged into the bath, and then they pass under the manipulations of the barber, and then they are taken to the wardrobe, and in the name of Him who said, "I was naked and ye clothed me," they are arrayed in appropriate attire, each one paying, if he can, so there shall be no sense of pauperism; some of them paying one penny for all the privileges of a bountiful table, and the most extravagant paying only six cents. Gymnasium to straighten and invigorate the pinched bodies. Books for the mind. Religion for the soul. I said, "Can these boys sing?" and the answer came back in an anthem that shook the room:

> Ring the bells of heaven,
> For there's joy to-day.

I said, "What is this long, broad box with so many numbers nailed by a great many openings?" "Oh," they said, "this is the savings bank; the boys put their money here, and each one has a bank-book, and he gets his money at the beginning of the month." Meanwhile, if under urgency for a new top, or attractive confectionery, or any one of those undefinable things which crowd a boy's pockets, he wants money, he cannot get it. He must wait until the first of the month, and so thrift and economy are cultivated. I know statistics are generally very dry, but here is a statistic which has in it as much spirit as anything that Thackeray ever wrote, and as much sublimity as anything John Milton ever wrote: One hundred and forty-three thousand boys have been assembled in these newsboys' lodging-houses since the establishment of the institution; twelve thousand have been returned to friends, and fifteen thousand have deposited in this great box over $42,000; while many of the lads have been prepared for usefulness, becoming farmers, mechanics, merchants, bankers, clergymen, lawyers, doctors, judges of courts even, and many of them prepared for heaven, where some have already entered, confronting, personally, that Christ in whose compassion the institution was established. And this society all the time transporting the lads to Western farms. No reformation for them while they stay in the dens of New York. What must be the sensation of a lad who has lived all his days in Elm street, or Water street, when he wakes up on the Iowa prairie, with one hundred miles room on all sides? One of these lads, getting out West, wrote a letter, descriptive of the place, and urging others to come. He said:

> "I am getting along first rate. I am on probation in the Methodist Church. I will be entered as a member the first of next month. I now teach a Sunday-school class of eleven boys. I get along first rate with it. This is a splendid country to make a living in. If the boys running around the street with a blacking-box on their shoulder or a bundle of papers under their arms only knew what high old times we boys have out here, they wouldn't hesitate about coming West, but come the first chance they got."

And to show the brightness of some of these lads, one of them made a little speech to his comrades just as he was about to start West, saying to his friends whom he was about to leave;

"Boys and gentlemen, perhaps you would like to hear sum'at about the West, the great West, you know, where so many of our old friends are settled down and going to be great men; some of the greatest men in the great Republic. Boys, that's the place for growing Congressmen, and Governors, and Presidents. Do you want to be newsboys always, and shoeblacks, and timber merchants in a small way, by selling matches? If you do, you will stay in New York; but if you don't, you will go out West and begin to be farmers; for the beginning of a farmer, my boys, is the making of a Congressman and a President. If you want to be loafers all your days, you will hang up your caps, and play around the groceries, and join fire engine and truck companies; but if you want to be the man who will make his mark in the country, you will get up steam and go ahead. There is lots of the prairies waiting for you. You havn't any idea of what you may be yet, if you will take a bit of my advice. How do you know but if you are honest and good and industrious, you may get so much up in the ranks that you will not have a general or a judge your boss? You will be lifted on horseback when you go to take a ride on the prairies, and if you choose to go in a wagon, or on an excursion, you will find that the hard times don't touch you there, and the best of all will be that if it is good to-day it will be better to-morrow."

Is not a lad like that worth saving? There are thousands of them in New York. God have mercy on them!

As I came down off the steps of that benevolent institution, I said, "Surely, the evils of our cities are not more wonderful than their charities." Then I started out through New Bowery, and I came to the sign of the Howard Mission, famous on earth and in heaven for the fact that through it so many Christian merchants and bankers, and philanthropists have saved multitudes of boys and girls from eternal calamity. Last summer that institution, taking some children one or two hundred miles into the country to be taken care of gratuitously for two or three weeks on farms, the train stopped at the depot, and one lad, who had never seen a green field, rushed out and gathered up the grass and the flowers, and came back and then took out a penny, his entire fortune, and handed it to the overseer, and said, "Here, take that penny and bring out more boys to see the flowers and the country." Seated on the platform of the Howard Mission that night, looking off upon these rescued children, I said within myself, "Who can estimate the reward for both worlds to these people who put their energies in such a Christ-like undertaking?" What a monument for Joseph Hoxie and Mr. Van Meter, the counselors of the institution in the past, and for A. S. Hatch and H. E. Tompkins, its advisers at the present, and thousands of people who in giving food through that institution have fed Christ, and in donating garments have clothed Christ, and in sheltering the wandering have housed Christ! God will pursue such men and women with His mercy to the edge of the pillow on which they die, and then, on the other side of the gate, He will give them a reception that will make all heaven echo and re-echo with their deeds. But oh! how much work—herculean, yea, omnipotent work—before all this vagrancy is ended! It is an authentic statistic that in this cluster of cities there are eighty thousand people over ten years of age who cannot write their names. Then what must be the ignorance of the multitudes under that age?

But I said to the driver, "We must hasten out on Broadway, for it is just the time when all the righteous and unrighteous places of amusement will be disbanding, and we shall see the people going up and down the streets. Coming from all sides, these are the great tides of life and death. The last orchestra had played. The curtain had dropped at the end of the play. The audiences of the concerts in the churches and the academies had all dispersed, moving up and down the street.

Good amusements are very good. Bad amusements are very bad. He who paints a fine picture, or who sculptures a beautiful statue, or sings a healthful song, or rouses an innocent laugh, or in any way cuts the strap of the burden of care on the world's shoulders, is a benefactor, and in the name of God I bless him; but between Canal street and Fourteenth street there are enough places of iniquitous amusement to keep all the world of darkness in perpetual holiday. In fifteen minutes, on any street almost of our city, you may find enough vicious amusement to invoke all the sulphur and brimstone that overwhelmed Sodom. The more than three hundred miles of Croton water pipes underlying New York city, emptied on these polluted places, could not wash them clean! You see the people coming out flushed with the strychnine wine taken in the recesses of the programme—some of the people in companionship that insures their present and eternal discomfiture, turning off from Broadway on the narrow streets running off either side! The recording angel shivered with horror as he penned their destiny.

Looking out of the carriage, I saw a tragedy on the corner of Broadway and Houston streets. A young man, evidently doubting as to which direction he had better take, his hat lifted high enough so you could see he had an intelligent forehead, stout chest; he had a robust development. Splendid young man. Cultured young man. Honored young man. Why did he stop there while so many were going up and down? The fact is, that every man has a good angel and a bad angel contending for the mastery of his spirit, and there was a good angel and a bad angel struggling with that young man's soul at the corner of Broadway and Houston streets. "Come with me," said the good angel; "I will take you home;

I will spread my wing over your pillow; I will lovingly escort you all through life under supernatural protection; I will bless every cup you drink out of, every couch you rest on, every doorway you enter; I will consecrate your tears when you weep, your sweat when you toil, and at the last I will hand over your grave into the hand of the bright angel of a Christian resurrection. In answer to your father's petition and your mother's prayer, I have been sent of the Lord out of heaven to be your guardian spirit. Come with me," said the good angel in a voice of unearthly symphony. It was music like that which drops from a lute of heaven when a seraph breathes on it. "No, no," said the bad angel, "come with me; I have something better to offer; the wines I pour are from chalices of bewitching carousal; the dance I lead is over floor tessellated with unrestrained indulgencies; there is no God to frown on the temples of sin where I worship. The skies are Italian. The paths I tread are through meadows, daisied and primrosed. Come with me." The young man hesitated at a time when hesitation was ruin, and the bad angel smote the good angel until it departed, spreading wings through the starlight upward and away until a door flashed open in the sky and forever the wings vanished. That was the turning point in that young man's history; for, the good angel flown, he hesitated no longer, but started on a pathway which is beautiful at the opening, but blasted at the last. The bad angel, leading the way, opened gate after gate, and at each gate the road became rougher and the sky more lurid, and what was peculiar, as the gate slammed shut it came to with a jar that indicated that it would never open. Passed each portal, there was a grinding of locks and a shoving of bolts; and the scenery on either side the road changed from gardens to deserts, and the June air became a cutting December blast, and the bright wings of the bad angel turned to sackcloth, and the eyes of light became hollow with hopeless grief, and the fountains, that at the start had tossed with wine, poured forth bubbling tears and foaming blood, and on the right side the road there was a serpent, and the man said to the bad angel, "What is that serpent?" and the answer was, "That is the serpent of stinging remorse." On the left side the road there was a lion, and the man asked the bad angel, "What is that lion?" and the answer was, "That is the lion of all-devouring despair." A vulture flew through the sky, and the man asked the bad angel, "What is that vulture?" and the answer was, "That is the vulture waiting for the carcasses of the slain." And then the man began to try to pull off of him the folds of something that had wound him round and round, and he said to the bad angel, "What is it that twists me in this awful convolution?" and the answer was, "That is the worm that never dies!" And then the man said to the bad angel, "What does all this mean? I trusted in what you said at the corner of Broadway and Houston streets; I trusted it all, and why have you thus deceived me?" Then the last deception fell off the charmer, and it said, "I was sent forth from the pit to destroy your soul; I watched my chance for many a long year; when you hesitated that night on Broadway I gained my triumph; now you are here. Ha! ha! You are here. Come, now, let us fill these two chalices of fire, and drink together to darkness and woe and death. Hail! Hail!" Oh! young man, will the good angel sent forth by Christ, or the bad angel sent forth by sin, get the victory over your soul? Their wings are interlocked this moment above you, contending for your destiny, as above the Apennines, eagle and condor fight mid-sky. This hour may decide your destiny. God help you. To hesitate is to die!

CHAPTER VII.

AMONG THIEVES AND ASSASSINS.

A certain man went down from Jerusalem to Jericho, and fell among thieves, which stripped him of his raiment and wounded him, and departed, leaving him half dead.—St. Luke x· 30.

This attack of highwaymen was in a rocky ravine, which gives to robbers a first-rate chance. So late as 1820, on that very road, an English traveler was shot and robbed. This wayfarer of the text not only lost his money and his apparel, but nearly lost his life. His assailants were not only thieves, but assassins. The scene of this lonely road from Jerusalem to Jericho is repeated every night in our great cities—men falling among thieves, getting wounded, and left half dead. In this series of Sabbath morning discourses on the night side of city life, as I have recently explored it, I have spoken to you of the night of pauperism, the night of debauchery and shame, the night of official neglect and bribery, and now I come to speak to you of the night of theft, the night of burglary, the night of assassination, the night of pistol and dirk and bludgeon. You say, what can there be in such a subject for me? Then you remind me of the man who asked Christ the question, "Who is my neighbor?" and in the reply of the text, Christ is setting forth the idea that wherever there is a man in trouble, there is your neighbor; and before I get through this morning, if the Lord will help me, I will show you that you have some very dangerous neighbors, and I will show you also what is your moral responsibility before God in regard to them.

I said to the chief official, "Give me two stout detectives for this night's work—men who are not only muscular, but who look muscular." I said to these detectives before we started on our midnight exploration, "Have you loaded pistols?" and they brought forth their firearms and their clubs, showing that they were ready for anything. Then I said, "Show me crime; show me crime in the worst shape, the most villainous and outrageous crime. In other words show me the worst classes of people to be saved by the power of Christ's gospel." I took with me only two officers of the law, for I want no one to run any risk in my behalf, and, having undertaken to show up the lowest depths of society, I felt I must go on until I had completed the work. One of the officers proposed to me that I take a disguise lest I be assailed. I said, "No; I am going on a mission of Christian work, and I am going to take the risks, and I shall go as I am." And so I went. You say to me, "Why didn't you first look after the criminal classes in Brooklyn?" I answer, it was not for any lack of material. Last year, in the city of Brooklyn, there were nearly 27,000 arrests for crime. Two hundred burglaries. Thirteen homicides. Twenty-seven highway robberies. Forty thousand lodgers in the station houses. Three hundred and thirty-six scoundrels who had their pictures taken for the Rogues Gallery, without any expense to those who sat for the pictures! Two hundred thousand dollars' worth of property stolen. Every kind of crime, from manslaughter to chicken thief. Indeed, I do not think there is any place in the land where you can more easily get your pocket picked, or your house burglarized, or your signature counterfeited, or your estate swindled, than in Brooklyn; but crime here is on a comparatively small scale, because we are a smaller city. The great depots of crime for this cluster of cities are in New York. It is a better hiding-place, the city is so vast, and all officers tell us that when a crime is committed in Jersey City, or is committed in Brooklyn, the villain attempts immediately to cross the ferry. While Brooklyn's sin is as enterprising as is possible for the number of inhabitants, crowd one million people on an island, and you have a stage and an audience on which and before whom crime may enact its worst tragedies.

There was nothing that more impressed me on that terrible night of exploration than the respect which crime pays to law when it is really confronted. Why do those eight or ten desperadoes immediately stop their blasphemy and their uproar and their wrangling? It is because an officer of the law calmly throws back the lappel of his coat and shows the badge of authority. The fact is that government is ordained of heaven, and just so far as the police officer does his duty, just so far is he a deputy of the Lord Almighty. That is the reason Inspector Murray, of New York, sometimes goes in and arrests four or five desperadoes. He is a man of comparatively slight stature, yet when one is backed up by omnipotent justice he can do anything. I said, "What is this glazed window, and who are these mysterious people going in and then coming out and passing down the street, looking to the pavement, and keeping a regular step until they hear a quick step behind them, and then darting down an alley?" This place, in the night of our exploration, was what the Bible calls "a den of thieves." They will not admit it. You cannot prove it against them, for the reason that the keeper and the patrons are the acutest men in the city. No sign of stolen goods, no loud talk about misdemeanors, but here a table surrounded by three or four persons whispering; yonder a table surrounded by three or four more persons whispering; before each man a mug of beer or stronger intoxicant. He will not drink to unconsciousness; he will only drink to get his courage up to the point of recklessness, all the while managing to keep his eye clear and his hand steady. These men around this table are talking over last night's exploit; their narrow escape from the basement door; how nearly they fell from the window-ledge of the second story; how the bullet grazed the hair. What is this bandaged hand you see in that room? That was cut by the window-glass as the burglar thrust his hand through to the inside fastening. How did that man lose his eye? It was destroyed three years ago by a premature flash of gunpowder in a store lock. Who are these three or four surrounding this other table? They are planning for to-night's villainy. They know just what hour the last member of the family will retire. They are in collusion with the servant, who has promised to leave one of the back windows open. They know at what time the man of wealth will leave his place of dissipation and start for home, and they are arranging it how they shall come out of the dark alley and bring him down with a slungshot. No sign of desperation in this room of thieves, and yet how many false keys, how many ugly pocket-knives, how many brass knuckles, how many revolvers! A few vulgar pictures on the wall, and the inevitable bar. Rum they must have to rest them after the exciting marauding. Rum they must have before they start on the new expedition of arson and larceny and murder. But not ordinary rum. It is poisoned four times. Poisoned first by the manufacturer; poisoned secondly by the wholesale dealer; poisoned thirdly by the retail dealer; poisoned fourthly by the saloon-keeper. Poisoned four times, it is just right to fit one for cruelty and desperation. These men have calculated to the last quarter of a glass how much they need to take to qualify them for their work. They must not take a drop too much nor a drop too little. These are the professional criminals of the city, between twenty-three and twenty-four hundred of them, in this cluster of cities. They are as thoroughly drilled in crime as, for good purposes, medical colleges train doctors, law colleges train lawyers, theological seminaries train clergymen. These criminals have been apprentices and journeymen; but now they are boss workmen. They have gone through the freshman, sophomore, junior and senior classes of the great university of crime, and have graduated with diplomas signed by all the faculty of darkness. They have no ambition for an easy theft, or an unskilled murder, or a blundering blackmail. They must have something difficult. They must have in their enterprise the excitement of peril. They must have something that will give them an opportunity of bravado. They must do something which amateurs in crime dare not do. These are the bank robbers, about sixty of them in this cluster of cities—men who somehow get in the bank during the daytime, then at night spring out upon the watchman, fasten him, and for the whole night have deliberate examination of the cashier's books to see whether he keeps his accounts correctly. These are the men who come in to examine the directory in the back part of your store while their accomplices are in the front part of the store engaging you in conversation, then dropping the directory and investigating the money safe. These are the forgers who get one of your canceled checks and one of your blank checks, and practice on the writing of your name until the deception is as perfect as the counterfeit check of Cornelius Vanderbilt, indorsed by Henry Keep, in 1870, for $75,000, which check was immediately cashed at the City Bank. These are the pickpockets, six hundred of them in this cluster of cities, who sit beside you in the stage and help you pass up the change! They stand beside you when you are shopping, and help you examine the goods, and weep beside you at the funeral, and sometimes bow their heads beside you in the house of God, doing their work with such adroitness that your affliction at the loss of the money is somewhat mitigated by your appreciation of the skill of the operator! The most successful of these are females, and, I suppose, on the theory that if a woman is good she is better than man, and if she is bad she is worse. She stands so much higher up than man that when she falls she falls further. Some of these criminals, pickpockets, and thieves also take the garb of clergymen. They look like doctors of divinity. With coats buttoned clear up to the chin, and white cravated, they look as if they were just going to pronounce the benediction, while they are all the time wondering where your watch is, or your portmonnaie is.

A thousand of the professional criminals do nothing but snatch things. They go in pairs, one of them keeping your attention in one part of the store, the other doing a lively business in another part of the store. At one end of the establishment the proprietor is smiling graciously on one who seems to be an exquisite lady, while in another part of the same establishment a roll of goods is taken up by a copartner in crime and put in a crocodile pocket, large enough to swallow everything. These professional criminals are the men who break in the windows of jewelry stores and snatch the jewels, and before the clerks have an opportunity of knowing what is the excitement are a block away, looking innocent, ready to come back and join in the pursuit of the offender, shouting with stentorian voice, "Stop, thief!" You wonder whether these people get large accumulation. No. Of the largest haul they get only a fifth, or a sixth, or a seventh part. It is the receiver of stolen goods that gets the profit. If these men during the course of their lives should get $50,000 they will live poor, and die poor, and be poor to all eternity. Among these professional criminals in our cities are the blackmailers—those who would have you pay a certain amount of money or have your character tarnished. If you are guilty I have no counsel to give in this matter; but if you are innocent let me say that no one of integrity need ever fear the blackmailer. All you have to do is to put the case immediately in the hands of Superintendent Walling of the New York police, or Superintendent Campbell of the Brooklyn police, and you will be vindicated. Depend upon it, however, that every dollar you pay to a blackmailer is toward your own everlasting enthrallment. A man in a cavern fighting a tigress might as well consent to give the tigress his right hand, letting her eat it up, with the supposition that she would let him off with the rest of his body, as for you to pay anything to a blackmailer with the idea of getting your character cleared. The thing to be done is to have the tigress shot, and that, the law is willing to do. Let me lay down a principle you can put in your memorandum books, and put in the front part of your Bible, and in the back part of your Bible, and put in your day-book, and put in your ledger—this principle: that no man's character is ever sacrificed until he sacrifices it himself. But you surrender your reputation, your fortune, your home, and your immortal soul, when you pay a farthing to a blackmailer.

Who are these men in this room at Hook Dock, or at the foot of Roosevelt street? They are professional criminals. Under the cover of the night they go down through the bay, or up and down the rivers. Finding two men in a row boat going to some steamer, or to one of the adjoining islands, they board the boat, rob the two men of their money, and, if they seem unreasonably opposed to giving up their money, taking their lives and giving them watery graves. These are the men who lounge around the solitary pier at night, and who clamber up on the side of the vessel lying at wharf, and, finding the captain asleep give him chloroform to help him sleep, and then knock the watchman overboard and take the valuables. Of this class were Howlett and Saul, who by twenty-one years of age had become the terror of the twenty-one miles of New York city water front, and who wound up their piracy by a murder on the bark "Thomas Watson," and crossed the gallows, relieving the world of their existence.

But in all these dens of thieves we find those who excite only our pity—people flung off the steeps of decent society. Having done wrong once, in despair they went to the bottom. Of such was that man who last Wednesday, in New York, stole a roll of goods, went to the station-house, said he was hungry, and asked to be sent to prison. Of such are those young men who make false entries in the account-book, resolved to "fix it up;" or who surreptitiously borrow from the commercial establishment, expecting to "fix it up;" but sickness comes, or accident comes, or a conjunction of unexpected circumstances, and they never "fix it up."

In disgrace they go down. Oh! how many, by force of

circumstances, and at the start with no very bad idea, get off the track and perish. A gentleman sitting in this assemblage this morning told me of an incident which occurred in a large commercial establishment, I believe the fourth in size in the whole country. The employer said to a young lady in the establishment, "You must dress better." She said, "I cannot dress better; I get $6 a week, and I pay $4 for my board, and I have $2 for dress and for my car fare; I cannot dress better." Then he said, "You must get it in some other way." Well, I suppose she could steal. I do not know how that incident affects you; but when it was told to me it made every drop of my blood, from scalp to heel, tingle with indignation. The fact is that there are thousands of men and women dropping into dishonesty and crime by force of circumstances, and by their destitution. Under the same kind of pressure you and I would have perished. It is despicable to stand on shore laughing at the shipwrecked struggling in the breakers when we ought to be getting out the rockets and the lifeboat and the ropes from the wrecking establishment. How much have you ever done to get this class ashore? In our city of Brooklyn we grip them of the police. Then we hustle them into a court room amid a great crowd of gaping spectators. Then we throw them into the worst jail on the continent—Raymond Street Jail. We put them in there with three or four confirmed criminals, and then actually deny $500 to the chaplain, who is giving his time for the alleviation of their condition, and putting our refusal of the $500 on the ground that if we support that thing in the penitentiary, and if we have religious services there it will be so much like uniting church and State!

"But," says some one at this point in my discourse,

"where does all this crime come from?" Let me tell you that New York is now paying for the political dishonesties of ten years ago. Do you believe that the political iniquities of 1868, 1869, 1870, and 1871 could be enacted in any city without demoralizing the community from top to bottom? Look at the sham elections of 1868 and 1869. Think of those times when a criminal was auditor of public accounts, and honorable gentlemen in the legal profession were put out of sight by shyster lawyers, and some of the police magistrates were worse than the criminals arraigned before them, and when the most notorious thief since the creation of the world, was a State Senator, holding princely levee at the Delevan House at Albany. Ah! my friends, those were the times when thousands of men were put on the wrong track. They said: "Why, what's the use of honest work when knavery declares such large dividends? What's the use of my going afoot in shoes I have to pay for myself, when I can have gilded livery sweeping through Broadway supported by public funds?" The rule was, as far as I remember it: Get an office with a large salary; if you cannot get an office with a large salary, get an office with a small salary, and then steal all you can lay your hands on, and call them "perquisites;" and then give subordinate offices to your friends, and let them help you on with the universal swindle, and get more "perquisites." Many of the young men of the cities were then eighteen years of age. They saw their parents hard at work with trowel and yardstick and pen, getting only a cramped living, while those men who were throwing themselves on their political wits had plenty of money and no work. Do you wonder that thousands adopted a life of dissipated indolence? Ten years having passed, they are now twenty-eight years of age, and in full swing of vagabondism. The putrid politics of ten years ago sowed much of the crop which is now being harvested by the almshouse and the penitentiary. But you say, "What is the practical use of this subject this morning? Have I any relation to it?" You have. In the last judgment you will have to give answer for your relation to it. Through all eternity you will feel the consequences of your relation to it. I could not waste my time, nor your time, in a discussion if there were not some practical significance to it. First of all, I give you a statistic which ought to make every office-table, and every counting-room desk, and every money-safe quake and tremble. It is the statistic that larcenies in New York city, directly and indirectly, cost that city $6,000,000 per year. There are all the moneys taken, in the first place. Then there are the prisons and the station-houses. Then there are the courts. Then there is the vast machinery of municipal government for the arraignment and treatment of villainy. Why, the Court of Sessions and the police courts cost the city of New York about $200,000 per year. The police force directly and indirectly costs the city of New York over $2,000,000 a year, and all that expenditure puts its tax on every bill of lading, on every yard of goods, on every parlor, every nursery, every store, every shop, every brick from foundation to capstone, every foot of ground from the south side of Castle Garden to the north side of Central Park, and upon all Brooklyn, and upon all Jersey City, for the reason that the interests of these cities are so interlocked that what is the prosperity of one is the prosperity of all, and what is the calamity of one is the calamity of all. But I do not, this morning, address you as financiers. I address you as moralists and Christian men and women, who before God have a responsibility for all this turpitude and scoundrelism, unless in every possible way you try to stop it and redeem it. "Oh!" says some one in the house, "such criminals as that cannot be reformed." I reply: Then you are stupidly ignorant of Christianity. Who was the man on the right-hand cross when Jesus was expiring? A thief—a dying thief. Where did he go to? To heaven. Christ said to him: "This day thou shalt be with me in Paradise." In that most conspicuous moment of the world's history, Christ demonstrating to all ages that the worst criminal can be saved. Who is that man in the Fourth Ward, New York, preaching the gospel every night of the week, and preaching it all the year round, and bringing more drunkards and thieves and criminals to the heart of a pardoning God than any twenty churches in Brooklyn or New York. Jerry McAuley, the converted river thief. That man took me to his front window the other evening, and he said, "Do you see that grog-shop over there?" I said, "Yes; I see it." "Well," he said, "I once was pitched out of that by the proprietor for being drunken and noisy. The grace of God has done a great deal for me. I was going along the street the other day, and that man who owned that groggery then, and who owns it now, wanted a favor of me, and he called to me. He did not call me drunken Jerry; but he said *Mister* McAuley—*Mister* McAuley!"

O! if the grace of God could do as much for that man it can save any outcast. If not, then what is the use of Paul's address when he says, "Let him that stole, steal no more"? I will tell you something—I do not care whether you like it or not—that at last, in heaven, there will be five hundred thousand converted thieves, pickpockets, gamblers, debauchees, murderers and outcasts, all saved by the grace of God, washed clean and prepared for glory. That exquisite out there gives a twitch to his kid glove, and that lady brings the skirt of her silk dress nearer her, as though she were afraid of having that truth tarnish her. "Why," says some one in the house, "are you going to make heaven such a common place as that?" I do not make it common. God makes it common. It is to be the most common place in the whole universe. By that I mean they are going to come up from all classes and conditions, and from the very lowest depths of society, washed clean by the grace of God, and entering heaven. "But," say some people, "what am I to do?" I will tell you three things, anyhow, you can do. First, avoid putting people in your employ amid too great temptation. You can take a young man in your employ and put him in a position where nine hundred and ninety-nine chances out of a thousand are that he will do wrong. Now, I say you have no right to do that. If you have any mercy on the criminal classes, and if you do not want to multiply their number, look out how you put people under temptation. In the second place, you can do this: you can speak a cheerful word when a man wants to reform. What chance is there for those who have gone astray? Here they are in the lowest depths of society, first of all, with their evil proclivities; then, with their evil associations. But suppose they conquer these evil proclivities, and break away from them. Now, they have come up to the door of society. Who will let them in? Will you? No; you dare not. They will go all around these doors of decent society, and find five hundred, and knock—no admittance; and knock—no admittance; and knock—no admittance. Now, I say it is your duty as a Christian man to help these people when they want to come up and come back. There is a third thing you can do, and that is, be the stanch friends of prison reform associations, home missionary societies, children's aid societies, and all those beneficent institutions which are trying to save our cities. But perhaps I ought to do my own work now, leaving yours for you to do some other time. I will now do that work. Very probably there is not in all this house one person who is known as a criminal, and yet I suppose there are scores of persons in this house who have done wrong. Now, perhaps I may meet their case healthfully and encouragingly when I tell them what I said to two young men. One young man said to me: "I have taken from my employer $2,500 in small amounts, but amounting to that. What shall I do?" I said, "Pay it back." He said, "I can't pay it back." Then I said, "Get your friends to help you pay it." He said, "I have no friends that will help me." Then I said, "I will give you two items of advice: First, go home and kneel down before God and ask his pardon. Then, to-morrow morning, when you go over to the store, get the head men of the firm in the private office, and tell them you have something very important to communicate, and let the door be locked. Then tell the whole story and ask their pardon. If they are decent men—not to say any thing about their being Christians or not Christians—if they are decent men, they will forgive you and help you to start again." "But," he said, "suppose they don't?" "Then," I said, "you have the Lord Almighty to see you through, and no man ever flung himself at Christ's feet but he was helped and delivered." Another young man came to me and said, "I have taken money from my employer. What shall I do?" I said, "Pay it back." "Well," he said, "I took a very large amount—I nearly paid it all back." I said, "Now, how long before you can pay it all back?" "Well," he said, "I can in two weeks, but my conscience disturbs me very much, and I want your counsel." It was a delicate case. I said to him, "You are sure you can pay it in two weeks?" "Yes; but," he said, "suppose I die?" I said to him: "If you can pay that all up, every farthing of it, in two weeks, pay it, and God don't ask you to disgrace yourself, or your family, and you won't die in two weeks. I see by the way you have been paying this up that you are going to be delivered. Ask God's pardon for what you have done, and never do so again."

It is very easy to be hard in making a rule, but I say the Gospel of Jesus Christ is a gospel of mercy, and wherever you find anybody in trouble, get him out. "Let the wicked forsake his way, and the unrighteous man his thoughts." You see, I am preaching a very practical sermon this morning. I know what are all the temptations of business life, and I did not come on this platform this morning to discourage anybody. I come to speak a word of good cheer to all the wandering and the lost, and I believe I am speaking it. The fact is, these cities are going to be redeemed. You know there is going to be another deluge. "Why," you say, "I thought the rainbow at the end of the great deluge, and the rainbow after every shower, was a sign that there would never be a deluge again!" But there will be another deluge. It will rain more than forty days and forty nights. The ark that will float that deluge will be immeasurably larger than Noah's ark, for it will hold a quadrillion of passengers. It will be the deluge of mercy, and the ark that floats that deluge will have five doors—one at the north to let in the frozen populations; one at the south to let in the sweltering and the sunburned; one at the east to let all China come in; one at the west, to let America in; one at the top, to let Christ, with all his flashing train of cherubim and archangel enter. And, as the rainbow of the ancient deluge gave sign that there would never be a deluge of destruction again, so the rainbow of this last deluge will give sign that the deluge will never depart. "For the knowledge of God shall cover the earth, as the waters cover the sea." Oh! ship of salvation, sail on. With all thy countless freight of immortals, put for the eternal shore. The thunders of the last day shall be the cannonade that will greet you into the harbor. Church triumphant, stretch down your arms of light across the gangway to welcome into port, church militant. "Hallelujah! for the Lord God omnipotent reigneth." Hallelujah! Amen!

CHAPTER VIII.

CLUB-HOUSES—LEGITIMATE AND ILLEGITIMATE.

Let the young men now arise and play before us.—II. Samuel ii: 14.

There are two armies encamped by the pool of Gibeon. The time hangs heavily on their hands. One army proposes a game of sword-fencing. Nothing could be more healthful and innocent. The other army accepts the challenge Twelve men against twelve men, the sport opens. But something went adversely. Perhaps one of the swordsmen got an unlucky clip, or in some way had his ire aroused, and that which opened in sportfulness ended in violence, each one taking his contestant by the hair, and then with the sword thrusting him in the side; so that that which opened in innocent fun ended in the massacre of all the twenty-four sportsmen. Was there ever a better illustration of what was true then, and is true now, that that which is innocent may be made destructive?

In my explorations of the night side of city life, I have found out that there is a legitimate and an illegitimate use of the club-house. In the one case it may become a heathful recreation, like the contest of the twenty-four men in the text when they began their play; in the other case it becomes the massacre of body, mind, and soul, as in the case of these contestants of the text when they had gone too far with their sport. All intelligent ages have had their gatherings for political, social, artistic, literary purposes—gatherings characterized by the blunt old Anglo-Saxon designation of "club." If you have read history, you know that there was a King's Head Club, a Ben Jonson Club; a Brothers' Club, to which Swift and Bolingbroke belonged; a Literary Club, which Burke and Goldsmith and Johnson and Boswell made immortal; a Jacobin Club, a Benjamin Franklin Junto Club. Some of these to indicate justice, some to favor the arts, some to promote good manners, some to despoil the habits, some to destroy the soul. If one will write an honest history of the clubs of England, Ireland, Scotland, France, and the United States for the last one hundred years, he will write the history of the world. The club was an institution born on English soil, but it has thrived well in American atmosphere. We have in this cluster of cities a great number of them, with seventy thousand members, so called, so known; but who shall tell how many belong to that kind of club where men put purses together and open house, apportioning the expense of caterer and servants and room, and having a sort of domestic establishment—a style of club-house which in my opinion is far better than the ordinary hotel or boarding-house? But my object now is to speak of club-houses of a different sort, such as the Union League, which was established during the war, having patriotic purposes, which has now between thirteen and fourteen hundred members, which is now also the headquarters of Republicanism; likewise the Manhattan, with large admission fee, four or five hundred members, the headquarters of the Democracy; like the Union Club, established in 1836, when New York had only a little over three hundred thousand inhabitants, their present building having cost $250,000—they have a membership of between eight and nine hundred people, among them some of the leading merchant princes of the land; like the Lotos, where journalists, dramatists, sculptors, painters and artists, from all branches, gather together to discuss newspapers, theatres, and elaborate art; like the Americus, which camps out in summer time, dimpling the pool with its hook and arousing the forest with its stag hunt; like the Century Club, which has its large group of venerable lawyers and poets; like the Army and Navy Club, where those who engaged in warlike service once on the land or the sea now come together to talk over the days of carnage; like the New York Yacht Club, with its floating palaces of beauty upholstered with velvet and paneled with ebony, having all the advantages of electric bell, and of gaslight, and of king's pantry, one pleasure-boat costing three thousand, another fifteen thousand, another thirty thousand, another sixty-five thousand dollars, the fleet of pleasure-boats belonging to the club having cost over two million dollars; like the American Jockey Club, to which belong men who have a passionate fondness for horses, fine horses, as had Job when, in the Scriptures, he gives us a sketch of that king of beasts, the arch of its neck, the nervousness of its foot, the majesty of its gait, the whirlwind of its power, crying out: "Hast thou clothed his neck with thunder? The glory of his nostrils is terrible; he paweth in the valley and rejoiceth in his strength, he saith among the trumpets ha! ha! and he smelleth the battle afar off, the thunder of the captains, and the shouting;" like the Travelers' Club, the Blossom Club, the Palette Club, the Commercial Club, the Liberal Club, the Stable Gang Club, the Amateur Boat Club, the gambling clubs, the wine clubs, the clubs of all sizes, the clubs of all morals, clubs as good as good can be, and clubs as bad as bad can be, clubs innumerable. No series of sermons on the night side of city life would be complete without a sketch of the clubs, which, after dark, are in full blast.

During the day they are comparatively lazy places. Here and there an aged man reading a newspaper, or an employee dusting a sofa, or a clerk writing up the accounts; but when the curtain of the night falls on the natural day, then the curtain of the club-house hoists for the entertainment. Let us hasten up, now, the marble stairs. What an imperial hallway! See! here are parlors on this side, with the upholstery of the Kremlin and the Tuilleries; and here are dining-halls that challange you to mention any luxury that they cannot afford; and here are galleries with sculpture, and paintings, and lithographs, and drawings from the best of artists, Cropsey, and Bierstadt, and Church, and Hart, and Gifford—pictures for every mood, whether you are impassioned or placid; shipwreck, or sunlight over the sea; Sheridan's Ride, or the noonday party of the farmers under the tree; foaming deer pursued by the hounds in the Adirondacks, or the sheep on the lawn. On this side there are reading-rooms where you find all newspapers and magazines. On that side there is a library, where you find all books, from hermeneutics to the fairy tale. Coming in and out there are gentlemen, some of whom stay ten minutes, others stay many hours. Some of these are from luxuriant homes, and they have excused themselves for a while from the domestic circle that they may enjoy the larger sociability of the club-house. These are from dismembered households, and they have a plain lodging somewhere, but they come to this club-room to have their chief enjoyment. One blackball amid ten votes will defeat a man's becoming a member. For rowdyism, for drunkenness, for gambling, for any kind of misdemeanor, a member is dropped out. Brilliant club-house from top to bottom. The chandeliers, the plate, the furniture, the companionship, the literature, the social prestige, a complete enchantment.

But the evening is passing on, and so we hasten through the hall and down the steps, and into the street. and from block to block until we come to another style of club-house. Opening the door, we find the fumes of strong drink and tobacco something almost intolerable. These young men at this table, it is easy to understand what they are at, from the flushed cheek, the intent look, the almost angry way of tossing the dice, or of moving the "chips." They are gambling. At another table are men who are telling vile stories. They are three-fourths intoxicated, and between 12 and 1 o'clock they will go staggering, hooting, swearing, shouting on their way home. That is an only son. On him all kindness, all care, all culture has been bestowed. He is paying his parents in this way for their kindness. That is a young married man, who, only a few months ago, at the altar, made promises of kindness and fidelity, every one of which he has broken. Walk through and see for yourself. Here are all the implements of dissipation and of quick death. As the hours of the night go away, the conversation becomes imbecile and more debasing. Now it is time to shut up. Those who are able to stand will get out on the pavement and balance themselves against the lamp-post, or against the railings of the fence. The young man who is not able to stand will have a bed improvised for him in the club-house, or two not quite so overcome with liquor will conduct him to his father's house, and they will ring the door-bell, and the door will open, and the two imbecile escorts will introduce into the hallway the ghastliest and most hellish spectacle that ever enters a front door—a drunken son. If the dissipating club-houses of this country would make a contract with the Inferno to provide it ten thousand men a year and for twenty years, on the condition that no more should be asked of them, the club-houses could afford to make that contract, for they would save homesteads, save fortunes, save bodies, minds, and souls. The ten thousand men who would be sacrificed by that contract would be but a small part of the multitude sacrificed without the contract. But I make a vast difference between clubs. I have belonged to four clubs: A theological club, a ball club, and two literary clubs. I got from them physical rejuvenation and moral health. What shall be the principle? If God will help me, I will lay down three principles by which you may judge whether the club where you are a member, or the club to which you have been invited, is a legitimate or an illegitimate club-house.

First of all I want you to test the club by its influences on home, if you have a home. I have been told by a prominent gentleman in club life that three-fourths of the members of the great clubs of these cities are married men. That wife soon loses her influence over her husband who nervously and foolishly looks upon all evening absence as an assault on domesticity. How are the great enterprises of art and literature and beneficence and public weal to be carried on if every man is to have his world bounded on one side by his front door-step, and on the other side by his back window, knowing nothing higher than his own attic, or nothing lower than his own cellar? That wife who becomes jealous of her husband's attention to art, or literature, or religion, or charity, is breaking her own sceptre of conjugal power. I know in this church an instance where a wife thought that her husband was giving too many nights to Christian service, to charitable service, to prayer meetings, and to religious convocation. She sytematically decoyed him away until now he attends neither this nor any other church, and is on a rapid way to destruction, his morals gone, his money gone, and, I fear, his soul gone. Let any Christian wife rejoice when her husband consecrates evenings to the service of God, or to charity, or to art, or to anything elevated; but let not men sacrifice home life to club life. I have the rolls of the members of a great many of the prominent clubs of these cities, and I can point out to you a great many names of men who are guilty of this sacrilege. They are as genial as angels at the club-house, and as ugly as sin at home. They are generous on all subjects of wine suppers, yachts, and fast horses, but they are stingy about the wife's dress and the children's shoes. That man has made that which might be a healthful recreation an usurper of his affections, and he has married it, and he is guilty of moral bigamy. Under this process the wife, whatever her features, becomes uninteresting and homely. He becomes critical of her, does not like the dress, does not like the way she arranges her hair, is amazed that he ever was so unromantic as to offer her hand and heart. She is always wanting money, money, when she ought to be discussing Eclipses, and Dexter, and Derby Day, and English drags with six horses, all answering the pull of one "ribbon."

I tell you, there are thousands of houses in Brooklyn and New York being clubbed to death! There are club-houses in these cities where membership always involves domestic shipwreck. Tell me that a man has joined a certain club, tell me nothing more about him for ten years, and I will write his history if he be still alive. The man is a wine-guzzler, his wife broken-hearted or prematurely old, his fortune gone or reduced, and his home a mere name in a directory. Here are six secular nights in the week. "What shall I do with them?" says the father and the husband. "I will give four of those nights to the improvement and entertainment of my family, either at home or in good neighborhood; I will devote one to charitable institutions; I will devote one to the club." I congratulate you. Here is a man who says, "I will make a different division of the six nights. I will take three for the club and three for other purposes." I tremble. Here is a man who says, "Out of the six secular nights of the week, I will devote five to the club-house and one to the home, which night I will spend in scowling like a March squall, wishing I was out spending it as I had spent the other five." That man's obituary is written. Not one out of ten thousand that ever gets so far on the wrong road ever stops. Gradually his health will fail, through late hours and through too much stimulus. He will be first-rate prey for erysipelas and rheumatism of the heart. The doctor coming in will at a glance see it is not only present disease he must fight, but years of fast living. The clergyman, for the sake of the feelings of the family, on the funeral day will only talk in religious generalities. The men who got his yacht in the eternal rapids will not be at the obsequies. They will have pressing engagements that day. They will send flowers to the coffin-lid, and send their wives to utter words of sympathy, but they will have engagements elsewhere. They never come. Bring me mallet and chisel, and I will cut on the tombstone that man's epitaph, "Blessed are the dead who die in the Lord." "No," you say, "that would not be appropriate." "Let me die the death of the righteous, and let my last end be like his." "No," you say, "that would not be appropriate." Then give me the mallet and the chisel, and I will cut an honest epitaph: "Here lies the victim of a dissipating club-house!" I think that damage is often done by the scions of some aristocratic family, who belong to one of these dissipating club-houses. People coming up from humbler classes feel it an honor to belong to the same club, forgetting the fact that many of the sons and grandsons of the large commercial establishments of the last generation are now, as to mind, imbecile; as to body, diseased; as to morals, rotten. They would have got through their property long ago if they had had full possession of it; but the wily ancestors, who got the money by hard knocks, foresaw how it was to be, and they tied up everything in the will. Now, there is nothing of that unworthy descendant but his grandfather's name and roast beef rotundity. And yet how many steamers there are which feel honored to lash fast that worm-eaten tug, though it drags them straight into the breakers.

Another test by which you can find whether your club is legitimate or illegitimate—the effect it has on your secular occupation. I can understand how through such an institution a man can reach commercial successes. I know some men have formed their best business relations through such a channel. If the club has advantaged you in an honorable calling it is a legitimate club. But has your credit failed? Are bargain-makers more cautious how they trust you with a bill of goods? Have the men whose names were down in the commercial agency A 1 before they entered the club, been going down since in commercial standing? Then look out! You and I every day know of commercial establishments going to ruin through the social excesses of one or two members. Their fortunes beaten to death with ball-players' bat, or cut amidships by the front prow of the regatta, or going down under the swift hoofs of the fast horses, or drowned in large potations of Cognac and Monongahela. Their club-house was the "Loch Earn." Their business house was the "Ville du Havre." They struck, and the "Ville du Havre" went under. Or, to take illustration from last Monday night's disaster: Their club-house was the "Eilion," and their business house was the "Pommerania." They struck, and the "Pommerania" went under.

A third test by which you may know whether the club to which you belong, or the club to whose membership you are invited, is a legitimate club or an illegitimate club, is this: What is its effect on your sense of moral and religious obligation? Now, if I should take the names of all the people in this audience this morning, and put them on a roll and then I should lay that roll back of this organ, and a hundred years from now some one should take that roll and call it from A to Z, there would not one of you answer. I say that any association that makes me forget that fact is a bad association. When I go to Chicago I am sometimes perplexed at Buffalo, as I suppose many travelers are, as to whether it is better to take the Lake Shore route or the Michigan Central, equally expeditious and equally safe, getting at the destination at the same time; but suppose that I hear that on one route the track is torn up, and the bridges are torn down, and the switches are unlocked? It will not take me a great while to decide which road to take. Now, here are two roads into the future, the Christian and the unchristian, the safe and the unsafe. Any institution or any association that confuses my idea in regard to that fact is a bad institution and a bad association. I had prayers before I joined the club. Did I have them after? I attended the house of God before I connected myself with the club. Since that union with the club do I absent myself from religious influences? Which would you rather have in your hand when you come to die, a pack of cards or a Bible? Which would you rather have pressed to your lips in the closing moment, the cup of Belshazzarean wassail or the chalice of Christian communion? Who would you rather have for your pall-bearers, the elders of a Christian church, or the companions whose conversation was full of slang and innuendo? Who would you rather have for your eternal companions, those men who spend their evenings betting, gambling, swearing, carousing, and telling vile stories, or your little child, that bright girl whom the Lord took? Oh! you would not have been away so much nights, would you, if you had known she was going away so soon? Dear me, your house has never been the same place since. Your wife has never brightened up. She has not got over it; she never will get over it. How long the evenings are, with no one to put to bed, and no one to tell the beautiful Bible story! What a pity it is that you cannot spend more evenings at home in trying to help her bear that sorrow! You can never drown that grief in the wine cup. You can never break away from the little arms that used to be flung around your neck when she used to say, "Papa, do stay home to-night—do stay home to-night." You will never be able to wipe from your lips the dying kiss of your little girl. The fascination of a dissipating club-house is so great that sometimes a man has turned his back on his home when his child was dying of scarlet fever. He went away. Before he got back at midnight the eyes had been closed, the undertaker had done his work, and the wife, worn out with three weeks watching, lay unconscious in the next room. Then there is a rattling of the night-key in the door, and the returned father comes up stairs, and he sees the cradle gone, and the windows up, and says, "What's the matter?" In the judgment day he will find out what was the matter. Oh! man astray, God help you! I am going to make a very stout rope. You know that sometimes a rope-maker will take very small threads, and wind them together until, after a while, they become ship-cable. And I am going to take some very small, delicate threads, and wind them together until they make a very stout rope. I will take all the memories of the marriage day, a thread of laughter, a thread of light, a thread of music, a thread of banqueting, a thread of congratulation, and I twist them together, and I have one strand. Then I take a thread of the hour of the first advent in your house, a thread of the darkness that preceded, and a thread of the light that followed, and a thread of the beautiful scarf that little child used to wear when she bounded out at eventide to greet you, and then a thread of the beautiful dress in which you laid her away for the resurrection. And then I twist all these threads together, and I have another strand. Then I take a thread of the scarlet robe of a suffering Christ, and a thread of the white raiment of your loved ones before the throne, and a string of the harp cherubic, and a string of the harp seraphic, and I twist them all together, and I have a third strand. "Oh!" you say, "either strand is strong enough to hold fast a world." No. I will take these strands, and I will twist them together, and one end of that rope I will fasten, not to the communion table for it shall be removed—not to a pillar of the organ, for that will crumble in the ages, but I wind it 'round and 'round the cross of a sympathizing Christ, and having fastened one end of the rope to the cross I throw the other end to you. Lay hold of it! Pull for your life! Pull for heaven!

CHAPTER IX.

POISON IN THE CALDRON.

"O thou man of God, there is death in the pot."—II. Kings iv: 40

Elisha had gone down to lecture to the theological students in the seminary at Gilgal. He found the students very hungry. Students are apt to be. In order that he might proceed with his lectures successfully, he sends out some servants to gather food for these hungry students. The servants are somewhat reckless in their work, and while they gather up some healthful herbs, they at the same time gather coloquintida, a bitter, poisonous, deathful weed, and they bring all the herbs to the house and put them in a caldron and stir them up, and then bring the food to the table, where are seated the students and their professor. One of the students takes some of the mixture and puts it to his lips, and immediately tastes the coloquintida, and he cries out to the professor: "O thou man of God, there is death in the pot." What consternation it threw upon the group. What a fortunate thing it was he found out in time, so as to save the lives of his comrades.

Well, there are now in the world a great many caldrons of death. The coloquintida of mighty temptations fills them. Some taste and quit, and are saved; others taste and eat on, and die. Is not that minister of Christ doing the right thing when he points out these caldrons of iniquity and cries the alarm, saying: "Beware! There is death in the pot"?

In a palace in Florence there is a fresco of Giotto

For many years that fresco was covered up with two inches thickness of whitewash, and it has only been in recent times that the hand of art has restored that fresco. "What sacrilege," you say, "to destroy the work of such a great master." But there is no sadness in that compared with the fact that the image of God in the soul has been covered up and almost obliterated so that no human hand can restore the Divine lineaments.

Iniquity is a coarse, jagged thing, that needs to be roughly handled. You have no right to garland it with fine phrase or lustrous rhetoric. You cannot catch a buffalo with a silken lasso. Men have no objections to having their sin looked at in a pleasant light. They will be very glad to sit for their photographs if you mak a handsome picture. But every Christian philanthropist must sometimes go forth and come in violent collision with transgression. I was in a whaling port, and I saw a vessel that had been on a whaling cruise come into the harbor, and it had patched sail and spliced rigging and bespattered deck, showing hard times and rough work. And so I have seen Christian philanthropists come back from some crusade against public iniquities. They have been compelled to acknowledge that it has not been yachting over summer lakes, but it has been outriding a tempest and harpooning great Behemoths.

A company of emigrants settle in a wild region. The very first day a beast from the mountains comes down and carries off one of the children, and the next day another beast comes and carries off another child. Forthwith all the neighbors band together, and with torch in one hand and gun in the other they go down into the caverns where those wild beasts are secreted, and slay them.

Now, my Christian friends, this morning I want to go

back of all public iniquity and find out its hiding-place. I want to know what are the sources of its power, or, to resume the figure of my text, I want to know what are the caldrons from which these iniquities are dipped out.

Unhappy and undisciplined homes *are the source of much iniquity.* A good home is deathless in its influences. Parents may be gone. The old homestead may be sold and have passed out of the possession of the family. The house itself may be torn down. The meadow brook that ran in front of the house may have changed its course or have dried up. The long line of old-fashioned sunflowers and the hedges of wild rose may have been graded, and in place thereof are now the beauties of modern gardening. The old poplar tree may have cast down its crown of verdure and may have fallen. You say you would like to go back a little while and see that home, and you go, and oh, how changed it is! Yet that place will never lose its charm over your soul. That first earthly home will thrill through your everlasting career. The dew-drops that you dashed from the chickweed as you drove the cows afield thirty years ago; the fire flies that flashed in your father's home on summer nights when the evenings were too short for a candle; the tinged pebbles that you gathered in your apron on the margin of the brook; the berries that you strung into a necklace, and the daisies that you plucked for your hair,—all have gone into your sentiments and tastes, and you will never get over them. The trundle bed where you slept; the chair where you sat; the blue-edged dish out of which you ate; your sister's skipping-rope; your brother's ball; your kite; your hoop; your mother's smile; your father's frown,—they are all part of the fibre of your immortal nature. The mother of missionary Schwartz threw light on the dusky brow of the savages to whom he preached long after she was dead. The mother of Lord Byron pursued him, as with a fiend's fury, into all lands, stretching gloom and death into "Childe Harold" and "Don Juan," and hovering in darkness over the lonely grave of Missolonghi.

Rascally and vagabond people for the most part come forth from unhappy homes. Parents harsh and cruel on the one hand, or on the other lenient to perfect looseness, are raising up a generation of vipers. A home in which scolding and fault-finding predominate is blood relation to the gallows and penitentiary. Petulance is a reptile that may crawl up into the family nest and crush it. There are parents who disgust their children even with religion. They scold their little ones for not loving God. They go about even their religious duties in an exasperating way. Their house is full of the war-whoop of contention, and from such scenes husbands and children dash out into places of dissipation to find their lost peace, or the peace they never had. O, is there some mother here, like Hagar, leading her Ishmael into the desert to be smitten of the thirst and parched in the sand? In the solemn birth-hour a voice fell straight from the skies into that dwelling, saying: "Take this child and nurse it for Me, and I will give thee thy wages." When angels of God at nightfall hover over that dwelling, do they hear the little ones lisp the name of Jesus? O, traveller for eternity, with your little ones gathered up under your robes, are you sure you are on the right road, or are you leading them on a dangerous and winding bridle path, off which their inexperienced feet may slip, and up which comes the howling of the wolf and the sound of loosening ledge and tumbling avalanche! Blessed the family altar where the children kneel. Blessed the cradle where the Christian mother rocks the Christian child. Blessed the song the little one sings at nightfall when sleep is closing the eyes and roosening the hand from the toy on the pillow. Blessed the mother's heart whose every throb is a prayer to God for the salvation of her children. The world grows old, and soon the stars will cease to illuminate it, and the herbage to clothe it, and the mountains to guard it, and the waters to refresh it, and the heavens to overspan it, and the long story of its sin, and shame, and glory, and triumph will turn into ashes; but parental influences, starting in the early home, will roll on and up into the great eternity, blooming in all the joy, waving in all the triumph, exulting in all the song of heaven, or groaning in all the pain, and shrinking back into all the shame, and frowning in all the darkness of the great prison house. O, father! O, mother! in which direction is your influence tending?

I verily believe that three-fourths of the wickedness of the great city runs out rank and putrid from undisciplined homes. Sometimes I know there is an exception. From a bright, beautiful, cheerful Christian home a husband or a son will go off to die. How long you have had that boy in your prayer. He does not know the tears you have shed. He knows nothing about the sleepless nights you have passed about him. He started on the downward road, and will not stop, call you never so tenderly. O, it is hard, it is very hard, after having expended so much kindness and care to get such pay of ingratitude. There is many a young man, proud of his mother, who would strike into the dust the dastard who would dare to do her wrong, whose hand this morning, by his first step in sin, is sharpening a dagger to plunge through that mother's heart. I saw it. The telegram summoned him. I saw him come in scarred and bloated, to look upon the lifeless form of his mother—those grey locks pushed back over the wrinkled brow he had whitened by his waywardness. Those eyes had rained floods of tears over his iniquity. That still, white hand had written many a loving letter of counsel and invitation. He had broken that old heart. When he came in he threw himself on the coffin and sobbed outright and cried: "Mother! mother!" but the lips that kissed him in infancy and that had spoken so kindly on other days when he came home, spake not. They were sealed forever. Rather than such a memory in my soul, I would have rolled on me now the Alps and the Himalayas. "The eye that mocketh its father, and refuseth to obey its mother, the ravens of the valley shall pick it out, and the young eagles shall eat it."

The second caldron of iniquity to which I point you is an indolent life. There are young men coming to our city with industrious habits, and yet they see in the city a great many men who seem to get along without any work. They have no business, and yet they are better dressed than industrious men, and they seem to have more facilities of access to amusements. They have plenty of time to spare to hang around the engine house, or the Pierrepont House, or the Saint Nicholas, or the other beautiful hotels; or lounge around the City Hall, their hands in their pockets, a tooth-pick in their mouth, waiting for some crumb to fall from the office-holder's table; or gazing at the criminals as they come up in the morning from the station-houses, jeering at them as they leap from the city van to the Court House steps. Ah, I would as soon think of standing at the gate of Greenwood to enjoy a funeral as to stand at the City Hall in the morning, when the city van drives up, to look at the carcasses of men and women slain for both worlds. The industrious people see these idlers standing about, and they wonder how they make their living. I wonder, too. They have plenty of money for the ride; they have plenty of money to bet on the boat race or the horse race; they can discuss the flavor of the costliest wines; they they have the best seats at Booth's Theater. But still you ask me: "How do they get their money?" Well, my friends, there are four ways of getting money—just four. By inheritance; by earning it; by begging it; by stealing it. Now, there are many people in our community who seem to have plenty of money, who did not inherit it, and who did not earn it, and who did not beg it. You must take the responsibility of saying how they got it. There are men who get tired of the drudgery of life, and see these prosperous idlers; and they consort with them, and they learn the same tricks, and they go to the same ruin—at death their departure causing no more mourning than is felt for the fast horse that they foundered and killed by a too hasty watering at "Tunison's." O, the pressure on the industrious young men is tremendous when they see people all around them full of seeming success but doing nothing. The multitude of those who get their living by sleight of hand is multiplying. What is the use of working in the store, or office, or shop, or on the scaffold, or by the forge, when you can get your living by your wits? A merchant in New York was passing along the street one evening, and he saw one of his clerks, half disguised, going into one of the low theaters. He said within himself: "I must look out for that young man." One morning the merchant came to his store, and this clerk of whom I have been speaking came up, in assumed consternation, and said: "The store has been on fire. I have got it put out; but many of the goods are gone." The merchant instantly seized the young man by the collar, and said: "I have had enough of this. You can't deceive me. Where are the goods you stole?" And the clerk confessed it instantly. The young man had gone into the plan of making money by sleight of hand and by his wits.

You will get out of this world just so much as, under God, you earn by your own hand and brain. Horatius was told he might have so much land as he could plough around in one day with a yoke of oxen, and I have noticed that men get nothing in this world, that is worth possessing, of a financial, moral, or spiritual nature, save they get it by their own hard work. It is just so much as, from the morning to the evening of your life, you can plough around by your own continuous and hard-sweating industries. "Go to the ant, thou sluggard, consider her ways, and be wise."

Another caldron of iniquity is the dram shop. Surely there is death in the pot. Anacharsis said that the vine had three grapes: pleasure, drunkenness, misery. Richard III. drowned his own brother Clarence in a butt of wine—these two incidents quite typical. Every saloon built above ground, or dug underground is a center of evil. It may be licensed, and for some time it may conduct its business in elegant style; but after awhile the cover will fall off, and you will see the iniquity in its right coloring. Plant a grog shop in the midst of the finest block of houses in your city, and the property will depreciate five, ten, twenty, thirty, fifty per cent. Men engaged in the ruinous traffic sometimes say: "You don't appreciate the fact that the largest revenues paid to the Government are by our business." Then I remember what Gladstone, the prime minister of England, said to a committee of men engaged in that traffic when they came to him to deplore that they were not treated with more consideration: "Gentlemen, don't be uneasy about the revenue. Give me thirty million sober people, and I will pay all the revenue, and have a large surplus." But, my friends, the ruin to property is a very small part of the evil. It takes everything that is sacred in the family, everything that is holy in religion, everything that is infinite in the soul, and tramples it into the mire.

The marriage day has come. The happy pair at the altar. The music sounds. The gay lights flash. The feet bound up and down the drawing-room. Started on a bright voyage of life. Sails all up. The wind is abaft. You prophesy everything beautiful. But the scene changes. A dingy garret. No fire. On a broken chair sits a sorrowing woman. Her last hope gone. Poor, disgraced, trodden underfoot—she knows the despair of being a drunkard's wife. The gay barque that danced off on the marriage morning has become a battered hulk, dismasted and shipwrecked. "O," she says, "he was as good a man as ever lived. He was so kind, he was so generous—no one better did God ever create than he; but the drink, the drink did it."

A young man starts from the country home for the city. Through the agency of metropolitan friends he has obtained a place in a store or a bank. That morning, in the farm house, the lights are kindled very early, and the boy's trunk is on the wagon. "I put a Bible in your trunk," says the mother, as she wipes the tears away with her apron. "My dear, I want you to read it when you get to town." "O," he says, "mother, don't you be worried about me. I know what I am about. I am old enough to take care of myself. Don't you be worried about me." The father says: "Be a good boy and write home often. Your mother will want to hear from you." Crack! goes the whip, and away over the hills goes the wagon. The scene changes. Five years after and there is a hearse coming up the old lane in front of the farm house. Killed in a porter house fight, that son has come home to disgrace the sepulchre of his fathers. When the old people lift the coffin lid, and see the changed face, and see the gash in the temples where the life oozed out, they will wring their withered hands and look up to heaven and cry: "*Cursed be rum!* CURSED BE RUM!"

Lorenzo de Medici was sick, and his friends thought that if they could dissolve some pearls in his cup, and then get him to swallow them, he would be cured. And so these valuable pearls were dissolved in his cup, and he drank them. What an expensive draught! But do you know that drunkenness puts into its cup the pearl of physical health, the pearl of domestic happiness, the pearl of earthly usefulness, the pearl of Christian hope, the pearl of an everlasting heaven, and then presses it to the lips? And oh, what an expensive draught! The dram shop is the gate of hell. While I speak there are some of you in the outer circles of this terrible maelstrom, and in the name of God I cry the alarm: "Put back now or never!" You say you are kind, and genial, and generous. I do not doubt it; but so much more the peril. Mean men never drink, unless some one else treats them. But the men who are in the front rank of this destructive habit are those who have a fine education, large hearts, genial natures and splendid prospects. This sin chooses the fattest lambs for sacrifice. What garlands of victory this carbuncled hand of drunkenness hath snatched from the brow of the orator and poet. What gleaming lights of generosity it has put out in midnight darkness. Come with me and look over—

come and hang over—look down into it while I lift off the cover, and you may see the loathsome, boiling seething, groaning, agonizing, blaspheming hell of the drunkard. There is everlasting death in the pot.

I have thought it might be appropriate at this season of the year, when we all mingle in hilarities, to warn our young friends not to put the cup of intoxication to their lips, and not to make these glorious seasons of family reunion and neighborhood congratulation the beginning of a long road of dissipation and sorrow. Young man! by the grace of God, be master of your appetites and passions. Frederick the Great, before he became "the Great," was seated with his roystering companions, and they were drinking, and hallooing, and almost imbecile, when word came to him that his father was dead, and consequently the crown was to pass to him. He rose up from among the boisterous crew, and stepped out and cried: "Stop your fooling; I am emperor!" Would to God that this day you might bring all your appetites and all your passions in subjection. "Better is he that ruleth his spirit than he that taketh a city." Be emperor! Yea, you are called this morning to be kings and to be priests unto God for ever. In the solemn hours of this closing year, and about to enter upon another year, if the Lord shall spare your lives for a few days longer, resolve that you will serve Him. Soon all the days and years of your life will have passed away, and then, the great eternity. "Rejoice, O, young man, in thy youth; let thy heart cheer thee in the days of thy youth, and walk thou in the sight of thine own eyes, and in the way of thine own heart; but know thou that for all these things God will bring thee into judgment."

CHAPTER X.

A CART-ROPE INIQUITY

"Woe unto them that sin as it were with a cart-rope."—Isaiah v: 18.

There are some iniquities that only nibble at the heart After a lifetime of their work, the man still stands upright, respected and honored. These vermin have not strength enough to gnaw through a man's character. But there are other transgressions that lift themselves up to gigantic proportions, and seize hold of a man and bind him with thongs for ever. There are some iniquities that have such great emphasis of evil that he who commits them may be said to sin as with a cart-rope. I suppose you know how they make a great rope. The stuff out of which it is fashioned is nothing but tow which you pull apart without any exertion of your fingers. This is spun into threads, any one of which you could easily snap, but a great many of these threads are interwound—then you have a rope strong enough to bind an ox, or hold a ship in a tempest. I speak to you of the sin of gambling. A cart-rope in strength is that sin, and yet I wish more especially to draw your attention to the small threads of influence out of which that mighty iniquity is twisted. This crime is on the advance, so that it is well not only that fathers, and brothers, and sons, be interested in such a discussion, but that wives, and mothers, and sisters, and daughters look out lest their present home be sacrificed, or their intended home be blasted. No man, no woman, can stand aloof from such a subject as this and say: "It has no practical bearing upon my life;" for there may be in a short time in your history an experience in which you will find that the discussion involved three worlds—earth, heaven, hell. There are in this cluster of cities about eight hundred confessed gambling establishments. There are about three thousand five hundred professional gamblers. Out of the eight hundred gambling establishments, how many of them do you suppose profess to be honest? Ten. These ten professing to be honest because they are merely the ante-chamber to the seven hundred and ninety that are acknowledged fraudulent. There are first-class gambling establishments. You step a little way out of Broadway. You go up the marble stairs. You ring the bell. The liveried servant introduces you. The walls are lavendar tinted. The mantles are of Vermont marble. The pictures are "Jephtha's Daughter," and Dore's "Dante's and Virgil's Frozen Region of Hell," a most appropriate selection, this last, for the place. There is the *roulette* table, the finest, costliest, most exquisite piece of furniture in the United States. There is the banqueting-room where, free of charge to the guests, you may find the plate, and viands, and wines, and cigars, sumptuous beyond parallel. Then you come to the second-class gambling-establishment. To it you are introduced by a card through some "roper in." Having entered, you must either gamble or fight. Sanded cards, dice loaded with quicksilver, poor drinks mixed with more poor drinks, will soon help you to get rid of all your money to a tune in short metre without staccato passages. You wanted to see. You saw. The low villains of that place watch you as you come in. Does not the panther, squat in the grass, know a calf when he sees it? Wrangle not for your rights in that place, or your body will be thrown bloody into the street, or dead into the East River.

You go along a little further and find the policy establishment. In that place you bet on numbers. Betting on two numbers is called a "saddle;" betting on three numbers is called a "gig;" betting on four numbers is called a "horse;" and there are thousands of our young men leaping into that "saddle," and mounting that "gig," and behind that "horse," riding to perdition. There is always one kind of sign on the door—"Exchange;" a most appropriate title for the door, for there, in that room, a man exchanges health, peace, and heaven, for loss of health, loss of home, loss of family, loss of immortal soul. Exchange sure enough and infinite enough.

Now you acknowledge that is a cart-rope of evil, but you want to know what are the small threads out of which it is made. There is, in many, a disposition to hazard. They feel a delight in walking near a precipice because of the sense of danger. There are people who go upon Jungfrau, not for the largeness of the prospect, but for the feeling that they have of thinking: "What would happen if I should fall off?" There are persons who have their blood filliped and accelerated by skating very near an air hole. There are men who find a positive delight in driving within two inches of the edge of a bridge. It is this disposition to hazard that finds development in gaming practices. Here are five hundred dollars. I may stake them. If I stake them I may lose them; but I may win five thousand dollars. Whichever way it turns, I have the excitement. Shuffle the cards. Lost! Heart thumps. Head dizzy. At it again—just to gratify this desire for *hazard*.

Then there are others who go into this sin through *sheer desire for gain*. It is especially so with professional gamblers. They always keep cool. They never drink enough to unbalance their judgment. They do not see the dice so much as they see the dollar beyond the dice, and for that they watch as the spider in the web, looking as if dead until the fly passes. Thousands of young men in the hope of gain go into these practices. They say: "Well, my salary is not enough to allow this luxuriance. I don't get enough from my store, office, or shop. I ought to have finer apartments. I ought to have better wines. I ought to have more richly flavored cigars. I ought to be able to entertain my friends more expensively. I wont stand this any longer. I can with one brilliant stroke make a fortune. Now, here goes, principle or no principle, heaven or hell. Who cares?" When a young man makes up his mind to live beyond his income, Satan has bought him out and out, and it is only a question of time when the goods are to be delivered. The thing is done. You may plant in the way all the batteries of truth and righteousness, that man is bound to go on. When a man makes one thousand dollars a year and spends one thousand two hundred dollars; when a young man makes one thousand five hundred dollars and spends one thousand seven hundred dollars, all the harpies of darkness cry out: "Ha! ha! we have him," and they have. How to get the extra five hundred dollars or the extra two thousand dollars is the question. He says: "Here is my friend who started out the other day with but little money, and in one night, so great was his luck, he rolled up hundreds and thousands of dollars. If he got it, why not I? It is such dull work, this adding up of long lines of figures in the counting-house; this pulling down of a hundred yards of goods and selling a remnant; this always waiting upon somebody else, when I could put one hundred dollars on the ace, and pick up a thousand." This sin works very insidiously.

Other sins sound the drum, and flaunt the flag, and

gather their recruits with wild huzza, but this marches its procession of pale victims in dead of night, in silence, and when they drop into the grave there is not so much sound as the click of a dice. O, how many have gone down under it. Look at those men who were once highly prospered. Now, their forehead is licked by a tongue of flame that will never go out. In their souls are plunged the beaks that will never be lifted. Swing open the door of that man's heart and you see a coil of adders wriggling their indescribable horror until you turn away and hide your face and ask God to help you to forget it. The most of this evil is unadvertised. The community does not hear of it. Men defrauded in gaming establishments are not fools enough to tell of it. Once in a while, however, there is an exposure, as when in Boston the police swooped upon a gaming establishment and found in it the representatives of all classes of citizens, from the first merchants on State street to the low Ann street gambler; as when Bullock, the cashier of the Central Railroad of Georgia, was found to have stolen one hundred and three thousand dollars for the purpose of carrying on gaming practices; as when a young man in one of the savings' banks of Brooklyn, many years ago, was found to have stolen forty thousand dollars to carry on gaming practices; as when a man connected with a Wall street insurance company was found to have stolen one hundred and eighty thousand dollars to carry on his gaming practices. But that is exceptional. Generally the money leaks silently from the merchant's till into the gamester's wallet. I believe that one of the main pipes leading to this sewer of iniquity is the excitement of business life. It is not a significant fact that the majority of the day gambling-houses in New York are in proximity to Wall street? Men go into the excitement of stock gambling, and from that they plunge into the gambling-houses, as, when men are intoxicated, they go into a liquor saloon to get more drink. The howling, screaming, stamping, Bedlamitish crew in the "Gold Room" drop into the gaming-houses to keep up their frenzy. The agitation that is witnessed in the stock market when the chair announces the word "North-western," or "Fort Wayne," or "Rock Island," or "New York Central," and the rat! tat! tat! of the auctioneer's hammer, and the excitement of making "corners," and getting up "pools," and "carrying stock," and a "break" from eighty to seventy, and the excitement of rushing about in curbstone brokerage, and the sudden cries of "Buyer three!" "Buyer ten!" "Take 'em!" "How many?" and the making or losing of ten thousand dollars by one operation, unfits a man to go home, and so he goes up the flight of stairs, amid business offices, to the darkly-curtained, wooden-shuttered room, gaily furnished inside, and takes his place at the *roulette* or the faro table. But I cannot tell all the process by which men get into this evil. One man came to our city of New York. He was a Western merchant. He went into a gaming-house on Park-place. Before morning he had lost all his money save one dollar, and he moved around about with that dollar in his hand, and after awhile, caught still more powerfully under the infernal infatuation, he came up and put down the dollar and cried out until they heard him through the saloon: "One thousand miles from home, and my last dollar on the gaming table."

Says some young man here this morning: "That cart-rope has never been wound around my soul." My brother, have not some threads of that cart-rope been twisted until after awhile they may become strong enough to bind you for ever?

I arraign before God the gift enterprises of our cities, which have a tendency to make this a nation of gamblers. Whatever you get, young man, in such a place as that, without giving a proper equivalent, is a robbery of your own soul, and a robbery of the community. Yet, how we are appalled to see men who have failed in other enterprises go into gift concerts, where the chief attraction is not music, but the prizes distributed among the audience; or to sell books where the chief attraction is not the book, but the package that goes with the book. Tobacco dealers advertise that on a certain day they will put money into their papers, so that the purchaser of this tobacco in Cincinnati or New York may unexpectedly come upon a magnificent gratuity. Boys hawking through the cars packages containing nobody knows what, until you open them and find they contain nothing. Christian men with pictures on their wall gotten in a lottery, and the brain of community taxed to find out some new way of getting things without paying for them. O, young men, these are the threads that make the cart rope, and when a young man consents to these practices, he is being bound hand and foot by a habit which has already destroyed "a great multitude that no man can number." Sometimes these gift enterprises are carried on in the name of charity; and you remember at the close of the late war how many gift enterprises were on foot, the proceeds to go to the orphans and the widows of the soldiers and sailors. What did the men who had charge of those gift enterprises care for the orphans and the widows? Why, they would have allowed them to freeze to death upon their steps. I have no faith in a charity which, for the sake of relieving present suffering, opens a gaping jaw that has swallowed down so much of the virtue and good principle of community. Young man, have nothing to do with these things. They only sharpen your appetite for games of chance. Do one of two things: be honest or die.

I have accomplished my object if I put the men in my audience on the look out. It is a great deal easier to fall than it is to get up again. The trouble is that when men begin to go astray from the path of duty, they are apt to say, "There's no use of my trying to get back. I've sacrificed my respectability, I can't return;" and they go on until they are utterly destroyed. I tell you, my friends, that God this moment, by His Holy Spirit, can change your entire nature, so that you will go out of this Tabernacle a far different man from what you were when you came in. Your great want—what is it? More salary? Higher social position? No; no. I will tell you the great want of every man in this house, if he has not already obtained it. It is the grace of God. Are there any here who have fallen victims to the sin that I have been reprehending? You are in a prison. You rush against the wall of this prison, and try to get out, and you fail; and you turn around and dash against the other wall until there is blood on the grates, and blood on your soul. You will never get out in this way. There is only one way of getting out. There is a key that can unlock that prison-house. It is the key of the house of David. It is the key that Christ wears at His girdle. If you will allow Him this morning to put that key to the lock, the bolt will shoot back, and the door will swing open, and you will be a free man in Christ Jesus. O, prodigal, what a business this is for you, feeding swine, when your father stands in the front door, straining his eyesight to catch the first glimpse of your return; and the calf is as fat as it will be, and the harps of heaven are all strung, and the feet free. There are converted gamblers in heaven. The light of eternity flashed upon the green baize of their billiard-saloon. In the laver of God's forgiveness they washed off all their sin. They quit trying for earthly stakes. They tried for heaven and won it. There stretches a hand from heaven toward the head of the worst man in all this audience. It is a hand, not clenched as if to smite, but outspread as if to drop a benediction. Other seas have a shore and may be fathomed, but the sea of God's love —eternity, has no plummet to strike the bottom, and immensity no iron-bound shore to confine it. Its tides are lifted by the heart of infinite compassion. Its waves are the hosannahs of the redeemed. The argosies that sail on it drop anchor at last amid the thundering salvo of eternal victory. But alas for that man who sits down to the final game of life and puts his immortal soul on the ace, while the angels of God keep the tally-board; and after the kings and queens, and knaves, and spades, are "shuffled" and "cut," and the game is ended, hovering and impending worlds discover that he has lost it, the faro-bank of eternal darkness clutching down into its wallet all the blood-stained wagers.

CHAPTER XI.

THE WOMAN OF PLEASURE.

She that liveth in pleasure is dead while she liveth.—I. Tim. v: 6

It is a strong way of putting the truth, that a woman who seeks in worldly advantage her chief enjoyment, will come to disappointment and death.

My friends, you all want to be happy. You have had a great many recipes by which it is proposed to give you satisfaction—solid satisfaction. At times you feel a thorough unrest. You know as well as older people what it is to be depressed. As dark shadows sometimes fall upon the geography of the school-girl as on the page of the spectacled philosopher. I have seen as cloudy days in May as in November. There are no deeper sighs breathed by the grandmother than by the granddaughter. I correct the popular impression that people are happier in childhood and youth than they ever will be again. If we live aright, the older we are the happier. The happiest woman that I ever knew was a Christian octogenarian; her hair white as white could be; the sunlight of heaven late in the afternoon gilding the peaks of snow. I have to say to a great many of the young people of this church that the most miserable time you are ever to have is just now. As you advance in life, as you come out into the world and have your head and heart all full of good, honest, practical, Christian work, then you will know what it is to begin to be happy. There are those who would have us believe that life is chasing thistle-down and grasping bubbles. We have not found it so. To many of us it has been discovering diamonds larger than the Kohinoor, and I think that our joy will continue to increase until nothing short of the everlasting jubilee of heaven will be able to express it.

Horatio Greenough, at the close of the hardest life a man ever lives—the life of an American artist—wrote: "I don't want to leave this world until I give some sign that, born by the grace of God in this land, I have found life to be a very cheerful thing, and not the dark and bitter thing with which my early prospects were clouded."

Albert Barnes, the good Christian, known the world over, stood in his pulpit in Philadelphia, at seventy or eighty years of age, and said: "This world is so very attractive to me, I am very sorry I shall have to leave it."

I know that Solomon said some very dolorous things about this world, and three times declared: "Vanity of vanities, all is vanity." I suppose it was a reference to those times in his career when his seven hundred wives almost pestered the life out of him! But I would rather turn to the description he has given of religion, when he says in another place: "Her ways are ways of pleasantness, and all her paths are peace." It is reasonable to expect it will be so. The longer the fruit hangs on the tree, the riper and more mellow it ought to grow. You plant one grain of corn, and it will send up a stalk with two ears, each having nine hundred and fifty grains, so that one grain planted will produce nineteen hundred grains. And ought not the implantation of a grain of Christian principle in a youthful soul develop into a large crop of gladness on earth and to a harvest of eternal joy in heaven? Hear me, then, this morning, while I discourse upon some of the mistakes which young people make in regard to happiness, and point out to the young women of this church what I consider to be the sources of complete satisfaction.

And, in the first place, I advise you *not to build your happiness upon mere social position.* Persons at your age, looking off upon life, are apt to think that if, by some stroke of what is called good-luck, you could arrive in an elevated and affluent position, a little higher than that in which God has called you to live, you would be completely happy. Infinite mistake! The palace floor of Ahasuerus is red with the blood of Vashti's broken heart. There have been no more scalding tears wept than those which coursed the cheeks of Josephine. If the sobs of unhappy womanhood in the great cities could break through the tapestried wall, that sob would come along your streets to-day like the simoon of the desert. Sometimes I have heard in the rustling of the robes on the city pavement the hiss of the adders that followed in the wake. You have come out from your home, and you have looked up at the great house, and covet a life under those arches, when, perhaps, at that very moment, within that house, there may have been the wringing of hands, the start of horror, and the very agony of hell. I knew such an one. Her father's house was plain, most of the people who came there were plain; but, by a change in fortune such as sometimes comes, a hand had been offered that led her into a brilliant sphere. All the neighbors congratulated her upon her grand prospects; but what an exchange! On her side it was a heart full of generous impulse and affection. On his side it was a soul dry and withered as the stubble of the field. On her side it was a father's house, where God was honored and the Sabbath light flooded the rooms with the very mirth of heaven. On his side it was a gorgeous residence, and the coming of mighty men to be entertained there; but within it were revelry and godlessness. Hardly had the orange blossoms of the marriage feast lost their fragrance, than the night of discontent began to cast here and there its shadow. The ring on the finger was only one link of an iron chain that was to bind her eternally captive. Cruelties and unkindness changed all those splendid trappings into a hollow mockery. The platters of solid silver, the caskets of pure gold, the head-dress of gleaming diamonds, were there; but no God, no peace, no kind words, no Christian sympathy. The festive music that broke on the captive's ear turned out to be a dirge, and the wreath in the plush was a reptile coil, and the upholstery that swayed in the wind was the wing of a destroying angel, and the bead-drops on the pitcher were the sweat of everlasting despair. O, how many rivalries and unhappinesses among those who seek in social life their chief happiness! It matters not how fine you have things; there are other people who have it finer. Taking out your watch to tell the hour of day, some one will correct your time-piece by pulling out a watch more richly chased and jeweled. Ride in a carriage that cost you eight hundred dollars, and before you get around the park you will meet with one that cost two thousand dollars. Have on your wall a picture by Copley, and before night you will hear of some one who has a picture fresh from the studio of Church or Bierstadt. All that this world can do for you in ribbons, in silver, in gold, in Axminster plush, in Gobelin tapestry, in wide halls, in lordly acquaintanceship, will not give you the ten-thousandth part of a grain of solid satisfaction. The English lord, moving in the very highest sphere, was one day found seated, with his chin on his hand, and his elbow on the window-sill, looking out, and saying: "O

I wish I could exchange places with that dog." Mere social position will never give happiness to a woman's soul. I have walked through the halls of those who despise the common people; I have sat at their banquets; I have had their friendship; yea, I have heard from their own lips the story of their disquietude; and I tell the young women of this church that they who build on mere social position their soul's immortal happiness, are building on the sand.

I go further, and advise you *not to depend for enjoyment upon mere personal attractions.* It would be sheer hypocrisy, because we may not have it ourselves, to despise, or affect to despise, beauty in others. When God gives it, He gives it as a blessing and as a means of usefulness. David and his army were coming down from the mountains to destroy Nabal and his flocks and vineyards. The beautiful Abigail, the wife of Nabal, went out to arrest him when he came down from the mountains, and she succeeded. Coming to the foot of the hill, she knelt. David with his army of sworn men came down over the cliffs, and when he saw her kneeling at the foot of the hill, he cried: "Halt!" to his men, and the caves echoed it: "Halt! halt!" That one beautiful woman kneeling at the foot of the cliff had arrested all those armed troops. A dew-drop dashed back Niagara. The Bible sets before us the portraits of Sarah and Rebecca, and Abishag, Absalom's sister, and Job's daughters, and says: "They were fair to look upon." By out-door exercise, and by skillful arrangement of apparel, let women make themselves attractive. The sloven has only one mission, and that to excite our loathing and disgust. But alas! for those who depend upon personal charms for their happiness. Beauty is such a subtle thing, it does not seem to depend upon facial proportions, or upon the sparkle of the eye, or upon the flush of the cheek. You sometimes find it among irregular features. It is the soul shining through the face that makes one beautiful. But alas! for those who depend upon mere personal charms. They will come to disappointment and to a great fret. There are so many different opinions about what are personal charms; and then sickness, and trouble, and age, do make such ravages. The poorest god that a woman ever worships is her own face. The saddest sight in all the world is a woman who has built everything on good looks, when the charms begin to vanish. O, how they try to cover the wrinkles and hide the ravages of time! When Time, with iron-shod feet, steps on a face, the hoof-marks remain, and you cannot hide them. It is silly to try to hide them. I think the most repulsive fool in all the world is an old fool!

Why, my friends, should you be ashamed to be getting old? It is a sign—it is *prima facie* evidence, that you have behaved tolerably well or you would not have lived to this time. The grandest thing, I think, is eternity, and that is made up of countless years. When the Bible would set forth the attractiveness of Jesus Christ, it says: "His hair was white as snow." But when the color goes from the cheek, and the lustre from the eye, and the spring from the step, and the gracefulness from the gait, alas! for those who have built their time and their eternity upon good looks. But all the passage of years cannot take out of one's face benignity, and kindness, and compassion, and faith. Culture your heart and you culture your face. The brightest glory that ever beamed from a woman's face is the religion of Jesus Christ. In the last war two hundred wounded soldiers came to Philadelphia one night, and came unheralded, and they had to extemporize a hospital for them, and the Christian women of my church, and of other churches, went out that night to take care of the poor wounded fellows. That night I saw a Christian woman go through the wards of the hospital, her sleeves rolled up, ready for hard work, her hair dishevelled in the excitement of the hour. Her face was plain, very plain; but after the wounds were washed and the new bandages were put round the splintered limbs, and the exhausted boy fell off into his first pleasant sleep, she put her hand on his brow, and he started in his dream, and said: "O, I thought an angel touched me!" There may have been no classic elegance in the features of Mrs. Harris, who came into the hospital after the "Seven Days" awful fight before Richmond, as she sat down by a wounded drummer-boy and heard him soliloquize: "A ball through my body, and my poor mother will never again see her boy. What a pity it is!" And she leaned over him and said: "Shall I be your mother, and comfort you?" And he looked up and said: "Yes, I'll try to think she's here. Please to write a long letter to her, and tell her all about it, and send her a lock of my hair and comfort her. But I would like to have you tell her how much I suffered—yes, I would like you to do that, for she would feel so for me. Hold my hand while I die." There may have been no classic elegance in her features, but all the hospitals of Harrison's Landing and Fortress Monroe would have agreed that she was beautiful; and if any rough man in all that ward had insulted her, some wounded soldier would have leaped from his couch, on his best foot, and struck him dead with a crutch.

Again: I advise you *not to depend for happiness upon the flatteries of men.* It is a poor compliment to your sex that so many men feel obliged in your presence to offer unmeaning compliments. Men capable of elegant and elaborate conversation elsewhere sometimes feel called upon at the door of the drawing-room to drop their common sense and to dole out sickening flatteries. They say things about your dress, and about your appearance, that you know, and they know, are false. They say you are an angel. You know you are not. Determined to tell the truth in office, and store, and shop, they consider it honorable to lie to a woman. The same thing that they told you on this side of the drawing-room, three minutes ago they said to some on the other side of the drawing-room. O, let no one trample on your self-respect. The meanest thing on which a woman can build her happiness is the flatteries of men.

Again: I charge you *not to depend for happiness upon the discipleship of fashion.* Some men are just as proud of being out of the fashion as others are of being in it. I have seen men as vain of their old fashioned coat, and their eccentric hat, as your brainless fop is proud of his dangling fooleries. Fashion sometimes makes a reasonable demand of us, and then we ought to yield to it. The daisies of the field have their fashion of color and leaf; the honeysuckles have their fashion of ear-drop; and the snowflakes flung out of the winter heavens have their fashion of exquisiteness. After the summer shower the sky weds the earth with ring of rainbow. And I do not think we have a right to despise all the elegancies and fashions of this world, especially if they make reasonable demands upon us; but the discipleship and worship of fashion is death to the body, and death to the soul. I am glad the world is improving. Look at the fashion plates of the seventeenth and eighteenth centuries, and you will find that the world is not so extravagant and extraordinary now as it was then, and all the marvellous things that the granddaughter will do will never equal that done by the grandmother. Go still further back to the Bible times, and you find that in those times fashion wielded a more terrible scepter. You have only to turn to the third chapter of Isaiah.

Only think of a woman having all that on! I am glad that the world is getting better, and that fashion which has dominated in the world so ruinously in other days has for a little time, for a little degree at any rate, relaxed its energies. Oh, the danger of the discipleship of fashion. All the splendors and the extravaganza of this world dyed into your robe and flung over your shoulder cannot wrap peace around your heart for a single moment. The gayest wardrobe will utter no voice of condolence in the day of trouble and darkness. That woman is grandly dressed, and only she, who is wrapped in the robe of a Savior's righteousness. The home may be very humble, the hat may be very plain, the frock may be very coarse; but the halo of heaven settles in the room when she wears it, and the faintest touch of the resurrection angel will change that garment into raiment exceeding white, so as no fuller on earth could whiten it. I come to you, young woman, to-day, to say that this world cannot make you happy. I know it is a bright world, with glorious sunshine, and golden rivers, and fire-worked sunset, and bird orchestra, and the darkest cave has its crystals, and the wrathiest wave its foam-wreath, and the coldest midnight its flaming aurora; but God will put out all these lights with the blast of his own nostrils, and the glories of this world will perish in the final conflagration. You will never be happy until you get your sins forgiven and allow Christ Jesus to take full possession of your soul. He will be your friend in every perplexity. He will be your comfort in every trial. He will be your defender in every strait. I do not ask you to bring, like Mary, the spices to the sepulcher of a dead Christ, but to bring your all to the feet of a living Jesus. His word is peace. His look is love. His hand is help. His touch is life. His smile is heaven. Oh, come, then, in flocks and groups! Come, like the south wind over banks of myrrh. Come, like the morning light tripping over the mountains. Wreathe all your affections for Christ's brow, set all your gems in Christ's coronet, pour all your voices into Christ's song, and let this Sabbath air rustle with the wings of rejoicing angels, and the towers of God ring out the news of souls saved!

"This world its fancied pearl may crave,
'Tis not the pearl for me;
'Twill dim its luster in the grave
'Twill perish in the sea.
But there's a pearl of price untold,
Which never can be bought with gold;
Oh, that's the pearl for me."

CHAPTER XII.

THE SINS OF SUMMER WATERING PLACES.

A pool, which is called in the Hebrew tongue Bethesda, having five porches. In these lay a multitude of blind, halt, withered, waiting for the moving of the water.—John v: 2, 3.

Outside of the city of Jerusalem, there was a sensitive watering-place, the popular resort for invalids. To this day, there is a dry basin of rock which shows that there must have been a pool there three hundred and sixty feet long, one hundred and thirty feet wide, and seventy-five feet deep. This pool was surrounded by five piazzas, or porches, or bathing-houses, where the patients tarried until the time when they were to step into the water. So far as reinvigoration was concerned, it must have been a Saratoga and a Long Branch on a small scale; a Leamington and a Brighton combined—medical and therapeutic. Tradition says that at a certain season of the year there was an officer of the government who would go down to that water and pour in it some healing quality, and after that the people would come and get the medication; but I prefer the plain statement of Scripture, that at a certain season, an angel came down and stirred up or troubled the water; and then the people came and got the healing. That angel of God that stirred up the Judean watering-place had his counterpart in the angel of healing that, in our day, steps into the mineral waters of Congress, or Sharon, or Sulphur Springs, or into the salt sea at Cape May and Nahant, where multitudes who are worn out with commercial and professional anxieties, as well as those who are afflicted with rheumatic, neuralgic, and splenetic diseases, go, and are cured by the thousands. These Bethesdas are scattered all up and down our country, blessed be God!

We are at a season of the year when railway trains are being laden with passengers and baggage on their way to the mountains, and the lakes, and the sea-shore. Multitudes of our citizens are packing their trunks for a restorative absence. The city heats are pursuing the people with torch and fear of sunstroke. The long silent halls of sumptuous hotels are all abuzz with excited arrivals. The crystalline surface of Winnipiseogee is shattered with the stroke of steamers laden with excursionists. The antlers of Adirondack deer rattle under the shot of city sportsmen. The trout make fatal snap at the hook of adroit sportsmen, and toss their spotted brilliance into the game basket. Soon the baton of the orchestral leader will tap the music-stand on the hotel green, and American life will put on festal array, and the rumbling of the tenpin alley, and the crack of the ivory balls on the green-baized billiard tables, and the jolting of the bar-room goblets, and the explosive uncorking of champagne bottles, and the whirl and the rustle of the ball-room dance, and the clattering hoofs of the race-courses, will attest that the season for the great American watering-places is fairly inaugurated. Music! Flute, and drum, and cornet-a-piston, and clapping cymbals, will wake the echoes of the mountains. Glad I am that fagged-out American life, for the most part, will have an opportunity to rest, and that nerves racked and destroyed will find a Bethesda.

I believe in watering-places. I go there sometimes. Let not the commercial firm begrudge the clerk, or the employer the journeyman, or the patient the physician, or the church its pastor, a season of inoccupation. Luther used to sport with his children; Edmund Burke used to caress his favorite horse; Thomas Chalmers, in the dark hour of the Church's disruption, played kite for recreation—so I was told by his own daughter—and the busy Christ said to the busy apostles: "Come ye apart awhile into the desert, and rest yourselves." And I have observed that they who do not know how to rest, do not know how to work.

But I have to declare this truth to-day, that some of our fashionable watering-places are the temporal and eternal destruction of "a multitude that no man can number;" and amid the congratulations of this season, and the prospect of the departure of many of you for the country, I must utter a note of warning, plain, earnest, and unmistakable. The first temptation that is apt to hover in this direction, is *to leave your piety all at home.* You will send the dog, and cat, and canary-bird to be well cared for somewhere else; but the temptation will be to leave your religion in the room with the blinds down and the door bolted, and then you will come back in the autumn to find that it is starved and suffocated, lying stretched on the rug, stark dead. There is no surplus of piety at the watering-places. I never knew any one to grow very rapidly in grace at the Catskill Mountain House, or Sharon Springs, or the Falls of Montmorency. It is generally the case that the Sabbath is more of a carousal than any other day, and there are Sunday walks, and Sunday rides, and Sunday excursions. Elders, and deacons, and ministers of religion, who are entirely consistent at home, sometimes when the Sabbath dawns on them at Niagara Falls, or the White Mountains, take the day to themselves. If they go to the church, it is apt to be a sacred parade, and the discourse, instead of being a plain talk about the soul, is apt to be what is called a crack sermon —that is, some discourse picked out of the effusions of the year as the one most adapted to excite admiration; and in those churches, from the way the ladies hold their fans, you know that they are not so much impressed with the heat as with the picturesqueness of half disclosed features. Four puny souls stand in the organ loft and squall a tune that nobody knows, and worshippers, with two thousand dollars worth of diamonds on the right hand, drop a cent into the poor-box, and then the benediction is pronounced, and the farce is ended. The toughest thing I ever tried to do was to be good at a watering.place.

The air is bewitched with the "world, the flesh, and devil." There are Christians who, in three or four weeks in such a place, have had such terrible rents made in their Christian robe, that they had to keep darning it until Christmas to get it mended! The health of a great many people makes an annual visit to some mineral spring an absolute necessity; but, my dear people, take your Bible along with you, and take an hour for secret prayer every day, though you be surrounded by guffaw and saturnalia. Keep holy the Sabbath, though they deride you as a bigoted Puritan. Stand off from John Morrissey's gambling hell, and those other institutions which propose to imitate on this side the water the iniquities of Baden-Baden. Let your moral and your immortal health keep pace with your physical recuperation and remember that all the waters of Hathorne, and sulphur and chalybeate springs cannot do you so much good as the mineral, healing, perrennial flood that breaks forth from the "Rock of Ages." This may be your last summer. If so, make it a fit vestibule of heaven.

Another temptation, however, around nearly all our watering-places, is *the horse-racing business.* We all admire the horse; but we do not think that its beauty, or speed, ought to be cultured at the expense of human degradation. The horse-race is not of such importance as the human race. The Bible intimates that a man is better than a sheep, and I suppose he is better than a horse, though, like Job's stallion, his neck be clothed with thunder.

Horse-races in olden times were under the ban of Christian people; and in our day the same institution has come up under fictitious names. And it is called a "Summer Meeting," almost suggestive of positive religious exercises. And it is called an "Agricultural Fair," suggestive of everything that is improving in the art of farming. But under these deceptive titles are the same cheating, and the same betting, and the same drunkenness, and the same vagabondage, and the same abominations that were to be found under the old horse-racing system. I never knew a man yet who could give himself to the pleasures of the turf for a long reach of time and not be battered in morals. They hook up their spanking team, and put on their sporting cap, and light their cigar, and take the reins, and dash down the road to perdition! The great day at Saratoga and Long Branch, and Cape May, and nearly all the other watering-places, is the day of the races. The hotels are thronged, every kind of equipage is taken up at an almost fabulous price; and there are many respectable people mingling with jockies and gamblers, and libertines, and foul-mouthed men and flashy women. The bar-tender stirs up the brandy smash. The bets run high. The greenhorns, supposing all is fair, put in their money, soon enough to lose it. Three weeks before the race takes place the struggle is decided, and the men in the secret know on which steed to bet their money. The two men on the horses riding around, long before arranged who shall beat. Leaning from the stand or from the carriage, are men and women so absorbed in the struggle of bone and muscle, and mettle, that they make a grand harvest for the pickpockets who carry off the pocket-books and portmonnaies. Men looking on see only two horses with two riders flying around the ring; but there is many a man on that stand whose honor, and domestic happiness, and fortune—white mane, white foot, white flank—are in the ring, racing with inebriety, and with fraud, and with profanity, and with ruin—black neck, black foot, black flank. Neck and neck, they go in that moral Epsom. White horse of honor; black horse of ruin. Death says: "I will bet on the black horse." Spectator says: "I will bet on the white horse." The white horse of honor a little way ahead. The black horse of ruin, Satan mounted, all the time gaining on him. Spectator breathless. Put on the lash. Dig in the spurs. There! They are past the stand. Sure. Just as I expected it. The black horse of ruin has won the race, and all the galleries of darkness "huzza! huzza!" and the devils come in to pick up their wagers. Ah, my friends, have nothing to do with horse-racing dissipations this summer. Long ago the English government got through looking to the turf for the dragoon and light cavalry horse. They found the turf depreciates the stock; and it is yet worse for men. Thomas Hughes, the member of Parliament, and the author known all the world over, hearing that a new turf enterprise was being started in this country, wrote a letter in which he said: "Heaven help you, then; for of all the cankers of our old civilization, there is nothing in this country approaching in unblushing meanness, in rascality holding its head high, to this belanded institution of the British turf." Another famous sportsman writes: "How many fine domains have been shared among these hosts of rapacious sharks during the last two hundred years; and unless the system be altered, how many more are doomed to fall into the same gulf!" The Duke of Hamilton, through his horse-racing proclivities, in three years got through his entire fortune of £70,000; and I will say that some of you are being undermined by it. With the bull-fights of Spain and the bear-baitings of the pit, may the Lord God annihilate the infamous and accursed horse-racing of England and America.

I go further and speak of another temptation that hovers over the watering place; and this is the *temptation to sacrifice physical strength.* The modern Bethesda, just like this Bethesda of the text, was intended to recuperate the physical health; and yet how many come from the watering-places, their health absolutely destroyed.

New York and Brooklyn idiots, boasting of having imbibed twenty glasses of congress water before breakfast. Families accustomed to going to bed at ten o'clock at night, gossiping until one or two o'clock in the morning. Dyspeptics, usually very cautious about their health, mingling ice-creams, and lemons, and lobster-salads, and cocoanuts until the gastric juices lift up all their voices of lamentation and protest. Delicate women and brainless young men chassezing themselves into vertigo and catalepsy. Thousands of men and women coming back from our watering-places in the autumn with the foundations laid for ailments that will last them all their life long. You know as well as I do that this is the simple truth. In the summer, you say to your good health: "Good-by; I am going to have a good time for a little while; I will be very glad to see you again in the autumn." Then in the autumn, when you are hard at work in your office, or store, or shop, or counting-room, Good Health will come in and say: "Good-by; I am going." You say: "Where are you going?" "O!" says Good Health, "I am going to take a vacation." It is a poor rule that will not work both ways, and your good health will leave you choleric, and splenetic, and exhausted. You coquetted with your good health in the summer-time, and your good health is coquetting with you in the winter-time. A fragment of Paul's charge to the jailer would be an appropriate inscription for the hotel register in every watering-place: "Do thyself no harm."

Another temptation hovering around the watering-place is to *the formation of hasty and life-long alliances.* The watering-places are responsible for more of the domestic infelicities of this country than all other things combined. Society is so artificial there that no sure judgment of character can be formed. They who form companionships amid such circumstances, go into a lottery where there are twenty blanks to one prize. In the severe tug of life you want more than glitter and splash. Life is not a ball-room, where the music decides the step, and bow, and prance, and graceful swing of long trail can make up for strong common sense. You might as well go among the gaily-painted yachts of a summer regatta to find war vessels, as to go among the light spray of the summer watering-place to find character that can stand the test of the great struggle of human life. Ah, in the battle of life you want a stronger weapon than a lace fan or a croquet mallet! The load of life is so heavy that in order to draw it you want a team stronger than one made up of a masculine grasshopper and a feminine butterfly. If there is any man in the community that excites my contempt, and that ought to excite the contempt of every man and woman, it is the soft-handed, soft-headed fop, who, perfumed until the air is actually sick, spends his summer in taking killing attitudes, and waving sentimental adieus, and talking infinitesimal nothings, and finding his heaven in the set of a lavender kid-glove. Boots as tight as an inquisition. Two hours of consummate skill exhibited in the tie of a flaming cravat. His conversation made up of "Ahs!" and "Ohs!" and "He-hes!" It would take five hundred of them stewed down to make a teaspoonful of calf's-foot jelly. There is only one counterpart to such a man as that, and that is the frothy young woman at the watering-place; her conversation made up of French moonshine; what she has on her head only equalled by what she has on her back; useless ever since she was born, and to be useless until she is dead; and what they will do with her in the next world I do not know, except to set her up on the banks of the River of Life, for eternity, to look sweet! God intends us to admire music, and fair faces and graceful step; but amid the heartlessness, and the inflation and the fantastic influences of our modern watering-places, beware how you make life-long covenants.

Another temptation that will hover over the watering-place is that to *baneful literature.* Almost every one starting off for the summer takes some reading matter. It is a book out of the library, or off the book-stand, or bought of the boy hawking books through the cars. I really believe there is more pestiferous trash read among the intelligent classes in July and August than in all the other ten months of the year. Men and women who at home would not be satisfied with a book that was not really sensible, I found sitting on hotel piazza, or under the trees, reading books, the index of which would make them blush if they knew that you knew what the book was. "O," they say, "you must have intellectual recreation." Yes. There is no need that you take along into a watering-place, "Hamilton's Metaphysics," or some thunderous discourse on the eternal decrees, or "Faraday's Philosophy." There are many easy books that are good. You might as well say: "I propose now to give a little rest to my digestive organs, and instead of eating heavy meat and vegetables, I will, for a little while, take lighter food—a little strychnine and a few grains of ratsbane." Literary poison in August is as bad as literary poison in December. Mark that. Do not let the frogs and the lice of a corrupt printing-press jump and crawl into your Saratoga trunk or White Mountain valise. Would it not be an awful thing for you to be struck with lightning some day when you had in your hand one of these paper-covered romances—the hero a Parisian *roue*, the heroine an unprincipled flirt—chapters in the book that you would not read to your children at the rate of a hundred dollars a line. Throw out all that stuff from your summer baggage. Are there not good books that are easy to read—books of entertaining travel; books of congenial history; books of pure fun; books of poetry, ringing with merry canto; books of fine engraving; books that will rest the mind as well as purify the heart and elevate the whole life? My hearers, there will not be an hour between this and the day of your death when you can afford to read a book lacking in moral principle.

Another temptation hovering all around our watering-places, is to *intoxicating beverage.* I am told that it is becoming more and more fashionable for women to drink; and it is not very long ago that a lady of great respectability, in this city, having taken two glasses of wine away from home, became violent, and her friends, ashamed, forsook her, and she was carried to a police station, and afterward to her disgraced home. I care not how well a woman may dress, if she has taken enough of wine to flush her cheek and put a glassiness on her eye, she is intoxicated. She may be handed into a 2500 dollar carriage, and have diamonds enough to confound the Tiffany's—she is intoxicated. She may be a graduate of Packer Institute, and the daughter of some man in danger of being nominated for the Presidency—she is drunk. You may have a larger vocabulary than I have, and you may say in regard to her that she is "convivial," or she is "merry," or she is "festive," or she is "exhilarated;" but you cannot, with all your garlands of verbiage, cover up the plain fact that it is an old-fashioned case of drunk. Now the watering-places are full of temptations to men and women to tipple. At the close of the ten-pin or billiard game, they tipple. At the close of the cotillion, they tipple. Seated on the piazza cooling themselves off, they tipple. The tinged glasses come around with bright straws, and they tipple. First, they take "light wines" as they call them; but "light wines," are heavy enough to debase the appetite. There is not a very long road between champagne at five dollars a bottle and whisky at five cents a glass. Satan has three or four grades down which he takes men to destruction. One man he takes up, and through one spree pitches him into eternal darkness. That is a rare case. Very seldom, indeed, can you find a man who will be such a fool as that. Satan will take another man to a grade, to a descent at an angle about like the Pennsylvania coal-shute, or the Mount Washington rail track, and shove him off. But that is very rare. When a man goes down to destruction, Satan brings him to a plane. It is almost a level. The depression is so slight that you can hardly see it. The man does not actually know that he is on the down grade, and it tips only a little toward darkness—just a little. And the first mile it is claret, and the second mile it is sherry, and the third mile it is punch, and the fourth mile it is ale, and the fifth mile it is porter, and the sixth mile it is brandy, and then it gets steeper, and steeper, and steeper, and the man gets frightened, and says: "O, let me get off." "No," says the conductor, "this is an express-train, and it don't stop until it gets to the Grand Central depot of Smashupton!" Ah, "Look not thou upon the wine when it is red, when it giveth its color in the cup, when it moveth itself aright. At the last it biteth like a serpent, and stingeth like an adder." And if any young man of my congregation should get astray this summer in this direction, it will not be because I have not given him fair warning.

My friends, whether you tarry at home—which will be quite as safe and perhaps quite as comfortable—or go into the country, arm yourself against temptation. The grace of God is the only safe shelter, whether in town or country. There are watering-places accessible to all of us. You cannot open a book of the Bible without finding out some such watering-place. Fountains open for sin and uncleanness. Wells of salvation. Streams from Lebanon. A flood struck out of the rock by Moses. Fountains in the wilderness discovered by Hagar. Water to drink and water to bathe in. The river of God which is full of water. Water of which if a man drink, he shall never thirst. Wells of water in the Valley of Baca.

Living fountains of water. A pure river of water as clear as crystal from under the throne of God. These are watering-places accessible to all of us. We do not have a laborious packing up before we start—only the throwing away of our transgressions. No expensive hotel bills to pay; it is "without money and without price." No long and dusty travel before we get there; it is only one step away. In California, in five minutes I walked around and saw ten fountains all bubbling up, and they were all different; and in five minutes I can go through this Bible *parterre* and find you fifty bright, sparkling fountains bubbling up into eternal life—healing and therapeutic. A chemist will go to one of these summer watering-places and take the water, and analyze it, and tell you that it contains so much of iron, and so much of soda, and so much of lime, and so much of magnesia. I come to this Gospel well, this living fountain, and analyze the water; and I find that its ingredients are peace, pardon, forgiveness, hope, comfort, life, heaven. "Ho, every one that thirsteth, come ye" to this watering-place. Crowd around this Bethesda this morning. O, you sick, you lame, you troubled, you dying—crowd around this Bethesda. Step in it, oh, step in it! The angel of the covenant this morning stirs the water! Why do you not step in it? Some of you are too weak to take a step in that direction. Then we take you up in the arms of our closing prayer, and plunge you clean under the wave, hoping that the cure may be as sudden and as radical as with Captain Naaman, who, blotched and carbuncled, stepped into the Jordan, and after the seventh dive came up, his skin roseate complexioned as the flesh of a little child.

CHAPTER XIII.

THE TIDES OF MUNICIPAL SIN.

He beheld the city, and wept over it.—Luke xix: 41.

The citizens of Old Jerusalem are in the tip-top of excitement. A country man has been doing some wonderful works and asserting very high authority. The police court has issued papers for his arrest, for this thing must be stopped, as the very government is imperilled. News comes that last night this stranger arrived at a suburban village, and that he is stopping at the house of a man whom he had resuscitated after four days' sepulture. Well, the people rush out into the streets, some with the idea of helping in the arrest of this stranger when he arrives, and others expecting that on the morrow he will come into the town, and by some supernatural force oust the municipal and royal authorities and take everything in his own hands. They pour out of the city gates until the procession reaches to the village. They come all around about the house where the stranger is stopping, and peer into the doors and windows that they may get one glimpse of him or hear the hum of his voice. The police dare not make the arrest because he has, somehow, won the affections of all the people. O, it is a lively night in Bethany. The heretofore quiet village is filled with uproar, and outcry, and loud discussion about the strange acting countryman. I do not think there was any sleep in that house that night where the stranger was stopping. Although he came in weary he finds no rest, though for once in his lifetime he had a pillow. But the morning dawns, the olive gardens wave in the light, and all along the road, reaching over the top of Olivet toward Jerusalem, there is a vast swaying crowd of wondering people. The excitement around the door of the cottage is wild, as the stranger steps out beside an unbroken colt that had never been mounted, and after his friends had strewn their garments on the beast for a saddle, the Saviour mounts it, and the populace, excited, and shouting, and feverish, push on back toward Jerusalem. Let none jeer now or scoff at this rider, or the populace will trample him under foot in an instant. There is one long shout of two miles, and as far as the eye can reach you see wavings of demonstrations and approval. There was something in the rider's visage, something in his majestic brow, something in his princely behavior, that stirs up the enthusiasm of the people. They run up against the beast and try to pull off into their arms, and carry on their shoulders, the illustrious stranger. The populace are so excited that they hardly know what to do with themselves, and some rush up to the roadside trees and wrench off branches and throw them in his way; and others doff their garments, what though they be new and costly, and spread them for a carpet for the conqueror to ride over. "Hosanna!" cry the people at the foot of the hill. "Hosanna!" cry the people all up and down the mountain. The procession has now come to the brow of Olivet. Magnificent prospect reaching out in every direction—vineyards, olive groves, jutting rock, silvery Siloam, and above all, rising on its throne of hills, the most highly honored city of all the earth, Jerusalem. Christ there, in the midst of the procession, looks off, and sees here fortressed gates, and yonder the circling wall, and here the towers blazing in the sun, Phasælus and Mariamne.

Yonder is Hippicus, the king's castle. Looking along in the range of the larger branch of that olive tree you see the mansions of the merchant princes. Through this cleft in the limestone rock you see the palace of the richest trafficker in all the earth. He has made his money by selling Tyrian purple. Behold now the Temple! Clouds of smoke lifting from the shimmering roof, while the building rises up beautiful, grand, majestic, the architectural skill and glory of the earth lifting themselves there in one triumphant doxology, the frozen prayer of all nations.

The crowd looked around to see exhilaration and transport in the face of Christ. O, no! Out from amid the gates, and the domes, and the palaces there arose a vision of that city's sin, and of that city's doom, which obliterated the landscape from horizon to horizon, and he burst into tears. "He beheld the city, and wept over it."

Standing in some high tower of the beloved city of our residence, we might look off upon a wondrous scene of enterprise, and wealth, and beauty; long streets faced by comfortable homes, here and there rising into affluence, while we might find thousands of people who would be glad to cast palm branches in the way of him who comes from Bethany to Jerusalem, greeting him with the vociferation: "Hosanna! to the Son of David." And yet how much there is to mourn over in our cities. Passing along the streets to-day are a great multitude. Whither do they go? To church. Thank God for that. Listen, this morning, and you hear multitudinous voices of praise. Thank God for that. When the evening falls you will find Christian men and women knocking at hovels of poverty, and finding no light, taking the matches from their pocket, and by a momentary glance revealing wan faces, and wasted hands, and ragged bed, sending in before morning, candles and vials of medicine, and Bibles and loaves of bread, and two or three flowers from the hot-house. Thank God for all that. But listen again, and you hear the thousand-voiced shriek of blasphemy tearing its way up from the depths of the city. You see the uplifted decanters emptied now, but uplifted to fight down the devils they have raised. Listen to that wild laugh at the street corner, that makes the pure shudder and say: "Poor thing, that's a lost soul!" Hark! to the click of the gambler's dice and the hysteric guffaw of him who has pocketed the last dollar of that young man's estate. This is the banquet of Bacchus. That young man has taken his first glass. That man has taken down three-fourths of his estate. This man is trembling with last night's debauch. This man has pawned everything save that old coat. This man is in delirium, sitting pale and unaware of anything that is transpiring about him—quiet until after awhile he rises up with a shriek, enough to make the denizens of the pit clap to the door and put their fingers in their ears, and rattle their chains still louder to drown out the horrible outcry. You say: "Is it not strange that there should be so much suffering and sin in our cities?" No, it is not strange. When I look abroad and see the temptations that are attempting to destroy men for time and eternity, I am surprised in the other direction that there are any true, upright, honest, Christian people left. There is but little hope for any man in these great cities who has not established in his soul, sound, thorough Christian principle.

First, look around you and see the temptations to commercial frauds. Here is a man who starts in business. He says: "I'm going to be honest;" but on the same street, on the same block, in the same business, are Shylocks. Those men, to get the patronage of any one, will break all understandings with other merchants, and will sell at ruinous cost, putting their neighbors at great disadvantage, expecting to make up the deficit in something else. If an honest principle could creep into that man's soul, it would die of sheer loneliness! The man twists about, trying to escape the penalty of the law, and despises God, while he is just a little anxious about the sheriff. The honest man looks about him and says: "Well, this rivalry is awful. Perhaps I am more scrupulous than I need be. This little bargain I am about to enter is a little doubtful; but then they all do it." And so I had a friend who started in commercial life, and as a book merchant, with a high resolve. He said: "In my store there shall be no books that I would not have my family read." Time passed on, and one day I went into his store and found some iniquitous books on the shelf, and I said to him: "How is it possible that you can consent to sell such books as these?" "Oh," he replied: "I have got over those puritanical notions. A man cannot do business in this day unless he does it in the way other people do it." To make a long story short, he lost his hope of heaven, and in a little while he lost his morality, and then he went into a mad-house. In other words, when a man casts off God, God casts him off.

One of the mightiest temptations in commercial life, in all our cities, to-day, is in the fact that many professed Christian men are not square in their bargains. Such men are in Baptist, and Methodist, and Congregational Churches, and our own denomination is as largely represented as any of them. Our good merchants are foremost in Christian enterprises; they are patronizers of art, philanthropic and patriotic. God will attend to them in the day of His coronation. I am not speaking of them, but of those in commercial life who are setting a ruinous example to our young merchants. Go through all the stores and offices in the city, and tell me in how many of those stores and offices are the principles of Christ's religion dominant? In three-fourths of them? No. In half of them? No. In one-tenth of them? No. Decide for yourself.

The impression is abroad, somehow, that charity can consecrate iniquitous gains, and that if a man give to God a portion of an unrighteous bargain, then the Lord will forgive him the rest. The secretary of a benevolent society came to me and said: "Mr. So-and-So has given a large amount of money to the missionary cause," mentioning the sum. I said: "I can't believe it." He said: "It is so." Well, I went home, staggered and confounded. I never knew the man to give to anything; but after awhile I found out that he had been engaged in the most infamous kind of an oil swindle, and then he proposed to compromise the matter with the Lord, saying: "Now, here is so much for Thee, Lord. Please to let me off!" I want to tell you that the Church of God is not a shop for receiving stolen goods, and that if you have taken anything from your fellows, you had better return it to the men to whom it belongs. If, from the nature of the circumstances, that be impossible, you had better get your stove red hot, and when the flames are at their fiercest, toss in the accursed spoil. God does not want it. The commercial world to-day is rotten through and through, and many of you know better than I can tell you that it requires great strength of moral character to withstand the temptations of business dishonesties. Thank God, a great many of you have withstood the temptations, and are as pure, and upright, and honest as the day when you entered business. But you are the exceptions in the case. God will sustain a man, however, amid all the excitements of business, if he will only put his trust in Him. In the drug-store, in Philadelphia, a young man was told that he must sell blacking on the Lord's day. He said to the head man of the firm: "I can't possibly do that. I am willing to sell medicines on the Lord's day, for I think that is right and necessary: but I can't sell this patent blacking." He was discharged from the place. A Christian man hearing of it, took him into his employ, and he went on from one success to another, until he was known all over the land for his faith in God and his good works, as well as for his worldly success. When a man has sacrificed any temporal, financial good for the sake of his spiritual interests, the Lord is on his side, and one with God is a majority.

Again: Look around you and see the pressure of political life. How many are going down under this influence. There is not one man out of a thousand that can stand political life in our cities. Once in awhile a man comes and says: "Now I love my city and my country, and, in the strength of God, I am going in as a sort of missionary to reform politics." The Lord is on his side. He comes out as pure as when he went in, and, with such an idea, I believe he will be sustained; but he is the exception. When such an upright, pure man does step into politics, the first thing, the newspapers take the job of blackening him all over, and they review all his past life, and distort everything that he has done, until, from thinking himself a highly respectable citizen, he begins to contemplate what a mercy it is that he has been so long out of gaol. The most hopeless, God-forsaken people in all our cities are those who, not in a missionary spirit, but with the idea of sordid gain, have gone into political life. I pray for the prisoners in gaol, and think they may be converted to God, but I never have any faith to pray for an old politician.

Then look around and see the allurements to an impure life. Bad books, unknown to father and mother, vile as the lice of Egypt, creeping into some of the best of families of the community; and boys read them while the teacher is looking the other way, or at recess, or on the corner of the street when the groups are gathered. These books are read late at night. Satan finds them a smooth plank on which he can slide down into perdition some of your sons and daughters. Reading bad books—one never gets over it. The books may be burned, but there is not enough power in all the apothecary's preparations to wash out the stain from the soul. Father's hands, mother's hands, sister's hands, will not wash it out. None but the hand of the Lord God can wash it out. And what is more perilous in regard to these temptations, we may not mention them. While God in this Bible, from chapter to chapter, thunders His denunciation against these crimes, people expect the pulpit and the printing-press to be silent on the subject, and just in proportion as people are impure are they fastidious on the theme. They are so full of decay and death they do not want their sepulchres opened. But I shall not be hindered by them. I shall go on in the name of the Lord Almighty, before whom you and I must at last come in judgment, and I shall pursue that vile sin, and thrust it with the two edged-sword of God's truth, though I find it sheltered under the chandeliers of some of your beautiful parlors. God will turn into destruction all the unclean, and no splendors of surrounding can make decent that which He has smitten. God will not excuse sin merely because it has costly array, and beautiful tapestry, and palatial residence, any more than He will excuse that which crawls, a blotch of sores, through the lowest cellar. Ever and anon, through some law-suit there flashes upon the people of our great cities what is transpiring in seemingly respectable circles. You call it "High life," you call it "Fast living," you call it "People's eccentricity." And while we kick off the sidewalk the poor wretch who has not the means to garnish his iniquity, these lords and ladies, wrapped in purple and fine linen, go unwhipped of public justice. Ah, the most dreadful part of the whole thing is that there are persons abroad whose whole business it is to despoil the young. Salaried by infamous establishments, these cormorants of darkness, these incarnate fiends, hang around your hotels, and your theatres, and they insinuate themselves among the clerks of your stores, and, by adroitest art, sometimes get in the purest circles. Oh, what an eternity such a man as that will have! As the door opens to receive him, thousands of voices will cry out: "See here what you have done;" and the wretch will wrap himself with fiercer flame and leap into deeper darkness, and the multitudes he has destroyed will pursue him, and hurl at him the long, bitter, relentless, everlasting curse of their own anguish. If there be one cup of eternal darkness more bitter than another, they will have to drink it to the dregs. If, in all the ocean of the lost world that comes billowing up, there be one wave more fierce than another, it will dash over them. "God will wound the hairy scalp of him who goeth on still in his trespasses."

I think you are persuaded there is but little chance

here in Brooklyn, or in New York, or Philadelphia, or Boston, for any young man without the grace of God. I will even go further and make it more emphatic, and say there is no chance for any young man who has not above him, and beneath him, and before him, and behind him, and on the right of him, and on the left of him, and within him, the all-protecting grace of God. My word of warning is to those who have recently come to the city; some of them entering our banking institutions, and some of them our stores and shops. Shelter yourselves in God. Do not trust yourselves an hour without the defences of Christ's religion.

I stood one day at Niagara Falls, and I saw what you may have seen there, six rainbows bending over that tremendous plunge. I never saw anything like it before or since. Six beautiful rainbows arching that great cataract! And so over the rapids and the angry precipices of sin, where so many have been dashed down, God's beautiful admonitions hover, a warning arching each peril—six of them, fifty of them—a thousand of them. Beware! beware! beware! This afternoon, young men, while you have time to reflect upon these things, and before the duties of the office and the store, and the shop come upon you again, look over this whole subject, and after the day has passed, and you hear in the nightfall the voices and the footsteps of the city dying from your ear, and it gets so silent that you can hear distinctly your watch under your pillow going "tick, tick!" then open your eyes, and look out upon the darkness, and see two pillars of light, one horizontal, the other perpendicular, but changing their direction until they come together, and your enraptured vision beholds it—THE CROSS!

CHAPTER XIV.

RESPONSIBILITY OF CITY RULERS.

O thou that art situate at the entry of the sea.—Ezek. xxvii: 3.

This is a part of an impassioned apostrophe to the city of Tyre. It was a beautiful city—a majestic city. At the east end of the Mediterranean, it sat with one hand beckoning the inland trade, and with the other the commerce of foreign nations. It swung a monstrous boom across its harbor to shut out foreign enemies, and then swung back that boom to let in its friends. The air of the desert was fragrant with the spices brought by caravans to her fairs, and all seas were cleft into foam by the keel of her laden merchantmen. Her markets were rich with horses, and mules, and camels from Togarmah; with upholstery, and ebony, and ivory from Dedan; with emeralds, and agate, and coral from Syria; with wine from Helbon; with finest needlework from Ashur and Chilmad. Talk about the splendid state-rooms of your White Star and French lines of international steamers. —why the benches of the state-rooms in those Tyrian ships were all ivory, and instead of our coarse canvas on the masts of the shipping, they had the finest linen, quilted together, and inwrought with embroideries almost miraculous for beauty. Its columns overshadowed all nations. Distant empires felt its heart beat. Majestic city! "situate at the entry of the sea."

But where now is the gleam of her towers, the roar of her chariots, the masts of her shipping? Let the fishermen who dry their nets on the place where she once stood; let the sea that rushes upon the barrenness where she once challenged the admiration of all nations; let the barbarians who build their huts on the place where her palaces glittered, answer the question. Blotted out for ever! She forgot God, and God forgot her. And while our modern cities admire her glory, let them take warning at her awful doom.

Cain was the founder of the first city, and I suppose it took after him in morals. It is a long while before a city can get over the character of those who founded it. Were they criminal exiles, the filth, and the prisons, and the debauchery are the shadows of such founders. New York will not for two or three hundred years escape from the good influences of its founders,—the pious settlers whose prayers went up from the very streets where now banks discount, and brokers shave, and companies declare dividends, and smugglers swear Custom-house lies; and above the roar of the drays, and the crack of auctioneers' mallets is heard the ascription—"We worship thee, O thou almighty dollar!" The church that once stood on Wall-street still throws its blessing over all the scene of traffic, and upon the ships that fold their white wings in the harbor. Originally men gathered in cities from necessity. It was to escape the incendiary's torch or the assassin's dagger. Only the very poor lived in the country, those who had nothing that could be stolen, or vagabonds who wanted to be near their place of business; but since civilization and religion have made it safe for men to live almost anywhere, men congregate in cities because of the opportunity for rapid gain. Cities are not necessarily evils, as has sometimes been argued. They have been the birth-place of civilization. In them popular liberty has lifted up its voice. Witness Genoa, and Pisa, and Venice. The entrance of the representatives of the cities in the legislatures of Europe was the death-blow to feudal kingdoms. Cities are the patronizers of art and literature,—architecture pointing to its British Museum in London, its Royal Library in Paris, its Vatican in Rome. Cities hold the world's sceptre. Africa was Carthage, Greece was Athens, England is London, France is Paris, Italy is Rome, and the cluster of cities in which God has cast our lot will yet decide the destiny of the American people.

The particular city in which God has given us a residence is under especial advantage. I may this morning apostrophize it in the words of my text, and say: "O thou that art situate at the entry of the sea!" Standing at the gates of the continent, we try to keep that which is worth keeping, and we try to pass on that which is of no use. The best pictures are in our galleries for exhibition, and foreign orators stop long enough to speak in our halls. The finest equipages may be seen on our Broadway, and making the circuit of our Central and Prospect Parks,—places fascinating with mosque, and fountains, and sculptured bridges, embowered walks, and menageries of wild animals, for the amusement of the people; while our Croton and Ridgewood aqueducts pour their brightness and refreshment into the hot lips of the thirsty cities. Thanking God this morning for the pleasant place in which He has cast our lot; and at this season of the year when so many of the offices of the city are changing hands, and so many new men are coming into positions of public trust, I have thought it might be useful to talk a little while about the moral responsibility resting upon the office-bearers in the city—a theme as appropriate to those who are governed as to the governors. The moral characters of those who rule a city has much to do with the character of the city itself. Men, women, and children are all interested in national politics. When the great Presidential election comes, every patriot wants to be found at the ballot box. We are all interested in the discussion of national reconstruction, national finance, national debt, and we read the laws of Congress, and we are wondering who will sit next in the Presidential chair. Now, that may be all very well—is very well; but it is high time that we took some of the attention which we have been devoting to national affairs and brought it to the study of municipal government. This it seems to me now is the chief point to be taken. Make the cities right, and the nation will be right. I have noticed that according to their opportunities there has really been more corruption in municipal governments in this country than in the State and national Legislatures. Now, is there no hope? With the mightiest agent in our hand, the glorious Gospel of Jesus Christ, shall not all our cities be reformed, and purified, and redeemed? I believe the day will come. I am in full sympathy with those who are opposed to carrying politics into religion; but our cities will never be reformed and purified until we carry religion into politics. I look over this city and I see that all our great interests are to be affected in the future, as they have been affected in the past, by the character of those who in the different departments rule over us, and I propose this morning to classify some of those interests.

In the first place I remark: Commercial ethics *are always affected by the moral or immoral character of those who have municipal supremacy.* Officials that wink at fraud, and that have neither censure nor arraignment for glittering dishonesties, always weaken the pulse of commercial honor. Every shop, every store, every bazaar, every factory in your city feels the moral character of your City Hall. If in any city there be a dishonest mayoralty, or an unprincipled Common Council, or a Court susceptible to bribes, in that city there will be unlimited license for all kinds of trickery and sin; while, on the other hand, if officials are faithful to their oath of office, if the laws are promptly executed, if there is vigilance in regard to the outbranchings of crime, there is the highest protection for all bargain making. A merchant may stand in his store and say: "Now I'll have nothing to do with city politics; I will not soil my hands with the slush;" nevertheless the most insignificant trial in the police court will affect that merchant directly or indirectly. What style of clerk issues the writ; what style of constable makes the arrest; what style of attorney issues the plea; what style of judge charges the jury; what style of sheriff executes the sentence—these are questions that strike your counting-rooms to the centre. You may not throw it off. In the city of New York Christian merchants for a great while said: "We'll have nothing to do with the management of public affairs," and they allowed everything to go at loose ends until there rolled up in that city a debt of nearly 120,000,000 dollars. The municipal government became a hissing and a by-word in the whole earth, and then the Christian merchants saw their folly, and they went and took possession of the ballot boxes. I wish all commercial men to understand that they are not independent of the moral character of the men who rule over them, but must be thoroughly, mightily affected by them.

So, also, of the educational interests of a city. Do you know that there are in this country sixty-five thousand common schools, and that there are over seven millions of pupils, and that the majority of those schools and the majority of those pupils are in our cities? Now, this great multitude of children will be affected by the intelligence or ignorance, the virtue or the vice, of Boards of Education and Boards of Control. There are cities—I am glad ours is not one of them—but there are cities where educational affairs are settled in the low caucus in the abandoned parts of the cities, by men full of ignorance and rum. It ought not to be so; but in many cities it is so. I hear the tramp of the coming generations. What that great multitude of youth shall be for this world and the next will be affected very much by the character of your public schools. You had better multiply the moral and religious influences about the common schools rather than subtract from them. Instead of driving the Bible out, you had better drive the Bible further in. May God defend our glorious common-school system, and send into rout and confusion all its sworn enemies!

I have also to say that *the character of officials in a city affects the domestic circle.* In a city where grog-shops have their own way, and gambling hells are not interfered with, and for fear of losing political influence officials close their eyes to festering abominations—in all those cities, the home interest need to make imploration. The family circles of the city must inevitably be affected by the moral character or the immoral character of those who rule over them.

I will go further and say that the religious interests of a city are thus affected. The church to-day has to contend with evils that the civil law ought to smite; and while I would not have the civil government in any wise relax its energy in the arrest and punishment of crime, I would have a thousand-fold more energy put forth in the drying up of the fountains of iniquity. The Church of God asks no pecuniary aid from political power; but does ask that in addition to all the evils we must necessarily contend against we shall not have to fight also municipal negligence. O, that in all our cities Christian people would rise up, and that they would put their hand on the helm before piratical demagogues have swamped the ship. Instead of giving so much time to national politics, give some of your attention to municipal government.

I am glad to know that recently our city has been cleansed of a great deal of political vermin, and yet it is not all gone. I see them still crawling around your City Hall—the disgust of all good men. Somehow, in the grinding of the political machine, they come on the top of the wheel. They electioneer hard at the polls, and they must have some crumbs of office or they will change their politics. The Democratic party would have us believe that that kind of men belong to the Republican party, and the Republican party would have us believe that that kind of men belong to the Democratic party. They are both wrong. They belong to both. It was well illustrated at the last election in New York City, where the two political parties, rousing themselves up to the fact that they ought to have some great reformer, some large-hearted reformer, some unimpeachable reformer—the two political parties joined together and elected to the Senatorial chair—John Morrissey! O, I demand that the Christian people who have been standing aloof from public affairs come back, and in the might of God try to save our cities. If things are or have been bad, it is because you have let them be bad. That Christian man who merely goes to the polls and casts his vote does not do his duty. It is not the ballot box that decides the election, it is the political caucus; and if at the primary meetings of the two political parties unfit and bad men are nominated, then the ballot box has nothing to do save to take its choice between two thieves! In our churches, by reformatory organization, in every way let us try to tone up the moral sentiment in these cities. The rulers are those whom the people choose, and depend upon it that in all the cities, as long as pure-hearted men stand aloof from politics because they despise hot partisanship, just so long in many of our cities will rum make the nominations, and rum control the ballot box, and rum inaugurate the officials.

I take a step further this morning, and I ask that all those of you who believe in the omnipotence of prayer, day by day, and every day, present your city officials before God for a blessing. *Pray for your mayor.* The chief magistrate of five hundred thousand souls is in a position of great responsibility. Many of the kings, and queens, and emperors of other days had no such dominion. With the scratch of a pen he may advance a beneficent institution or baulk an elevated steam railway confiscation. By appointments he may bless or curse every hearthstone in the city. If in the Episcopal churches, by the authority of the Litany, and in our non-Episcopate churches, we every Sabbath pray for the President of the United States, why not, then, be just as hearty in our supplications for the chief magistrate of our cities, for their guidance, for their health, for their present and everlasting morality?

But go further, and *pray for your Common Council.* They hold in their hands a power splendid for good or terrible for evil. They have many temptations. In many of the cities whole Boards of Common Councilmen have gone down in the maelstrom of political corruption. They could not stand the power of the bribe. Corruption came in and sat beside them, and sat behind them, and sat before them. They recklessly voted away the hard-earned moneys of the people. They were bought out, body, mind and soul, so that at the end of their term of office they had not enough of moral remains left to make a decent funeral. They went into office with the huzza of the multitude. They came out with the anathema of all decent people. There is not one man out of a hundred that can endure the temptations of the Common Councilmen in our great cities. And if a man in that position have the courage of a Cromwell, and the independence of an Andrew Jackson, and the public spiritedness of a John Frederick Oberlin, and the piety of an Edward Payson, he will have no surplus to throw away. Pray for these men. Every man likes to be prayed for. Do you know how Dr. Norman McLeod became the Queen's chaplain? It was by a warm-hearted prayer in the Scotch kirk, in behalf of the Royal Family, one Sabbath when the Queen and her son were present *incognito.*

Yes, go further, my friends, and *pray for your police.* Their perils, and temptations, best known to themselves. They hold the order and the peace of your city in their grasp. But for their intervention you would not be safe for an hour. They must face the storm. They must rush in where it seems to them almost instant death. They must put the hand of arrest on the armed maniac, and corner the murderer. They must refuse large rewards for withdrawing complaints. They must unravel intricate plots, and trace dark labyrinths of crime, and develop suspicions into certainties. They must be cool while others are frantic. They must be vigilant while others are somnolent, impersonating the very villainy they want to seize. In the police forces of our great cities are to-day men of as thorough character as that of the old detective of New York, addressed to whom there came letters from London asking for help ten years after he was dead—letters addressed to "Jacob Hayes, High Constable of New York." Your police need your appreciation, your sympathy, your gratitude, and, above all, your prayers. And there is no church more indebted to that class of men than this. When, last year, we were arraigning some public iniquities, and the wrath of all the powers of darkness seemed to be stirred up, the police came in—not at our invitation, but voluntarily—and sixty of them sat in every service in this church, for six weeks, that there might be neither interruption nor bloodshed. We thank them. We sympathize with them. We pray for them.

Yea, I want you to go further, and *pray every day for your prison inspectors and your jail-keepers,*—work awful and beneficent. Rough men, cruel men, impatient men, are not fit for those places. They have under their care men who were once as good as you, but they got tripped up. Bad company, or strong drink, or a strange conjunction of circumstances, flung them headlong. Go down that prison corridor and ask them how they got in, and about their families, and what their early prospects in life were, and you will find that they are very much like yourself, except in this: that God kept you while He did not restrain them. Just one false step made the difference between them and you. They want more than prison bars, more than jail fare, more than handcuffs and hopplers, more than a vermin-covered couch to reform them. Pray God, day by day, that the men who have these unfortunates in charge may be merciful, Christianly strategic, and the means of reformation and rescue. Some years ago a city pastor in New York was called to the city prison to attend a funeral.

A young woman had committed a crime, and was incarcerated, and her mother came to visit her, and died on the visit. The mother, having no home, was buried from her daughter's prison-cell. After the service was over, the imprisoned daughter came up to the minister of Christ, and said: "Wouldn't you like to see my poor mother?" And while they stood at the coffin, the minister of Christ said to that imprisoned soul: "Don't you feel to-day, in the presence of your mother's dead body, as if you ought to make a vow before God that you will do differently and live a better life?" She stood for a few moments, and then the tears rolled down her cheeks, and she pulled from her right hand the worn-out glove that she had put on in honor of the obsequies, and, having bared her right hand, she put it upon the chill brow of her dead mother, and said: "By the help of God I swear I will do differently. God help me." And she kept her vow. And years after, when she was told of the incident, she said: "When that minister of the Gospel said: 'God bless you and help you to keep the vow that you have made,' I cried out, and I said: 'You bless me! Do you bless me? Why, that's the first kind word I've heard in ten years;' and it thrilled through my soul, and it was the means of my reformation, and ever since, by the grace of God, I've tried to live a Christian life." O yes, there are many amid the criminal classes that may be reformed. Pray for the men who have these unfortunates in charge; and who knows but that, when you are leaving this world, you may hear the voice of Christ dropping to your dying pillow, saying: "I was sick and in prison, and you visited me." Yea, I take the suggestion of the Apostle Paul, and ask you to pray for all who are in authority, that we may lead quiet and peaceable lives in godliness and honesty.

My word this morning now is to all in this assembly and to those whom these words shall come who hold any public position of trust in our midst. You are God's representatives. God the King, and Ruler, and Judge, sets you in His place. O, be faithful in the discharge of all your duties, so that when Brooklyn is in ashes, and the world itself is a red scroll of flame, you may be in the mercy and grace of Christ rewarded for your faithfulness. It was that feeling which gave such eminent qualifications for office to Neal Dow, Mayor of Portland, and to Judge McLean, of Ohio, and to Benjamin F. Butler, Attorney-General of New York, and to George Briggs, Governor of Massachusetts, and to Theodore Frelinghuysen, Senator of the United States, and to William Wilberforce, member of the British Parliament. You may make the rewards of eternity the emoluments of your office. What care you for adverse political criticism if you have God on your side! The one, or the two, or the three years of your public trust will pass away, and all the years of your earthly service, and then the tribunal will be lifted, before which you and I must appear. May God make you so faithful now that the last scene shall be to you exhilaration and rapture. I wish this morning to exhort all good people, whether they are the governors or the governed, to make one grand effort for the salvation, the purification, the redemption of Brooklyn. Do you not know that there are multitudes going down to ruin, temporal and eternal, dropping quicker than words drop from my lips? Grog-shops swallow them up. Gambling hells devour them. Houses of shame are damning them. O, let us toil, and pray, and preach, and vote until all these wrongs are righted. What we do we must do quickly. Soon you will not sit there, and I will not stand here. With our rulers, and on the same platform, we must at last come before the throne of God to answer for what we have done for the bettering of the condition of the five hundred thousand people in Brooklyn. Alas! if on that day it be found that your hand has been idle and my pulpit has been silent. O, ye who are pure, and honest, and Christian, go to work and help me to make this city pure, and honest, and Christian.

Lest it may have been thought that I am this morning preaching only to what are called the better classes, my final word is to some dissolute soul that has strayed here to-day. Though you may be covered with all crimes, though you may be smitten with all leprosies, though you may have gone through the whole catalogue of iniquity, and may not have been in church for twenty years before to-day—before you leave this house you may have your nature entirely reconstructed, and upon your brow, hot with infamous practices and besweated with exhausting indulgences, God will place the flashing coronet of a Saviour's forgiveness. "O, no!" you say, "if you knew who I am and where I came from this morning, you wouldn't say that to me. I don't believe the Gospel you are preaching speaks of my case." Yes it does, my brother. And then when you tell me that, I think of what St. Teresa said when reduced to utter destitution, having only two pieces of money left, she jingled the two pieces of money in her hand and said: "St. Teresa and two pieces of money are nothing; but St, Teresa and two pieces of money and God are all things." And I tell you to-day that while a sin and a sinner are nothing, a sin and a sinner and an all-forgiving and all-compassionate God are everything.

Who is that that I see coming? I know his step. I know his rags. Who is it? A prodigal. Come, people of God, let us go out and meet him. Get the best robe you can find in all this house. Let the angels of God fill their chalices and drink to his eternal rescue. Come, people of God, let us go out to meet him. The prodigal is coming home. The dead is alive again, and the lost is found. Hallelujah!

"Pleased with the news, the saints below
In songs their tongues employ;
Beyond the skies the tidings go,
And Heaven is filled with joy.

"Nor angels can their joy contain,
But kindle with new fire;
'The sinner lost is found,' they sing,
And strike the sounding lyre."

CHAPTER XV.

SAFEGUARDS OF YOUNG MEN.

"Is the young man Absalom safe?"—II. Sam. xviii: 29.

The heart of David, the father, was wrapped up in his boy Absalom. He was a splendid boy, judged by the rules of worldy criticism. From the crown of his head to the sole of his foot there was not a single blemish. The Bible says that he had such a luxuriant shock of hair, that when once a year it was shorn, what was cut off weighed over three pounds. But, notwithstanding all his brilliancy of appearance, he was a bad boy, and broke his father's heart. He was plotting to get the throne of Israel. He had marshalled an army to overthrow his father's government. The day of battle had come. The conflict was begun. David, the father, sat between the gates of the palace waiting for the tidings of the conflict. Oh, how rapidly his heart beat with emotion. Two great questions were to be decided: the safety of his boy, and the continuance of the throne of Israel. After awhile, a servant, standing on the top of the house, looks off, and he sees some one running. He is coming with great speed, and the man on the top of the house announces the coming of the messenger, and the father watches and waits, and as soon as the messenger from the field of battle comes within hailing distance the father cries out. Is it a question in regard to the establishment of his throne? Does he say: "Have the armies of Israel been victorious? Am I to continue in my imperial authority? Have I overthrown my enemies?" Oh! no. There is one question that springs from his heart to the lip, and springs from the lip into the ear of the besweated and bedusted messenger flying from the battle-field—the question, "Is the young man Absalom safe?" When it was told to David, the King, that, though his armies had been victorious, his son had been slain, the father turned his back upon the congratulations of the nation, and went up the stairs of his palace, his heart breaking as he went, wringing his hands sometimes, and then again pressing them against his temples as though he would press them in, crying: "O Absalom! my son! my son! Would God I had died for thee, O Absalom! my son! my son!"

My friends, the question which David, the King, asked in regard to his son is the question that resounds to-day in the hearts of hundreds of parents. Yea, there are a great multitude of young men here who know that the question of the text is appropriate when asked in regard to them. They know the temptations by which they are surrounded; they see so many who started life with as good resolutions as they have who have fallen in the path, and they are ready to hear me ask the question of my text: "Is the young man Absalom safe?" The fact is that this life is full of peril. He who undertakes it without the grace of God and a proper understanding of the conflict into which he is going must certainly be defeated. Just look off upon society to-day. Look at the shipwreck of men for whom fair things were promised, and who started life with every advantage. Look at those who have dropped from high social position, and from great fortune, disgraced for time, disgraced for eternity. To prove that this life is an awful peril unless a man has the grace of God to defend him, I point to that wreck of Friday at Ludlow street Jail, showing on what a desolate coast a strong craft may crash and part. Let there be no exhilaration over that man's fate. Instead of the chuckle of satisfaction, let there be in every Christian soul a deep sadness. The fact is, that there are tens of thousands of men in this country who, under the same pressure of temptation, would have fallen as low. Instead of bragging and boasting how you have maintained your integrity, you had better get down on your knees and thank God that His Almighty grace has kept you from the same moral catastrophe. There is no advice more appropriate to you and this whole country this morning than the advice of the Scripture, which says: "Let him that standeth take heed lest he fall." All my sympathies are for the afflicted family of that dead prisoner. For the last seven years some of them I know have endured an inquisition of torture. May the God of all comfort help them in this day when there are so few to pray for them. In the presence of this Christian assemblage I invoke the God of all compassion to have mercy upon those bereft children. It is hard to see our friends die, even when they die in Christian triumph and with all blissful surroundings; but alas! when to the natural anguish is added the anguish of a moral and a lifetime shipwreck. Ah! my friends, let us remember that that man made full expiation to society for his crimes against it. Let us remember that by pangs of body that no doctor could arrest, and by horrors of soul which no imagination can describe, he fully paid the price of his iniquity. Let others do as they may, I will not throw one nettle or one thistle on that man's grave. But, my friends, no minister of religion, no man who stands as I do, Sabbath morning and Sabbath night and Friday night, before a great multitude of young men, trying to help them and educate them for time and eternity, can allow that event of the past week to go by without drawing from it a lesson of the fact that life is an awful peril without the religion of Jesus Christ, and that "the way of the transgressor is hard." No stouter nature ever started out on this world than William M. Tweed. He conquered poverty; he conquered lack of education; he achieved an aldermanic chair in the metropolis of this country; he gained a position in the Congress at Washington, and then he took his position on a financial throne of power at Albany, his frown making legislative assemblages tremble, while he divided the notoriety with James Fisk, Jr., of being the two great miscreants of the nineteenth century. Alas! Alas! Young man, look at the contrast—in elegant compartment of Wagner's palace-car, surrounded by wines and cards and obsequious attendants, going to the Senatorial place in Albany; then look again at the plain box in the undertaker's wagon at three o'clock of last Friday at the door of a prison. Behold the contrast—the pictured and bouqueted apartments at the Delavan, liveried servants admitting millionaires and Senators who were flattered to take his hand; then see the almost friendless prisoner on a plain cot, throwing out his dying hand to clutch that of Luke, his black attendant. Behold the wedding party at the mansion, the air bewitched with crowns, and stars, and harps of tuberoses and japonicas; among the wedding presents, forty complete sets of silver; fifteen diamond sets, one set of diamonds worth $45,000; the wedding dress at the expense of $4,000, with trimmings that cost another $1,000; two baskets of silverware, representing icebergs, to contain the ices, while Polar bears of silver lie down on the handles of the baskets; the banquet, the triumph of

Delmonico's lifetime; the whole scene a bewilderment of costliness and magnificence. And then behold the low-ceiling room, looking out on a dingy street, where poor, exhausted, forsaken, betrayed, sick William M. Tweed lies a dying. From how high up to how low down! There were many common people in New York who for years were persuaded by what they saw that an honest and laborious life did not pay. As the carriage swept by containing the jewelled despoiler of public funds, men felt like throwing their burdens down and trying some other way of getting a livelihood; but where is the clerk on $500 salary a year, where is the porter who will to-morrow sweep out the store, where is the scavenger of the street who would take Tweed's years of fraudulent prosperity if he must also take Tweed's sufferings, and Tweed's dishonor, and Tweed's death? Ah! there never was such an illustration for the young men of New York and Brooklyn of the fact that dishonesty will not pay. Take a dishonest dollar and bury it in the centre of the earth, and heap all the rocks of the mountain on the top of it; then cover these rocks with all the diamonds of Golconda, and all the silver of Nevada, and all the gold of California and Australia, put on the top of these all banking and moneyed institutions, and they cannot keep down that one dishonest dollar. That one dishonest dollar in the centre of the earth will begin to heave and rock and upturn itself until it comes to the resurrection of damnation. "As a partridge sitteth on eggs and hatcheth them not, so riches got by fraud, a man shall leave them in the midst of his days, and at the end he shall be a fool." You tell me that in the last days the man of whom I speak read his Bible three times a day. I cast no slur on such a thing as that. It was beautiful, and it was appropriate. God could save that man as easily as He could save you or me. Had I been called to do so, I should have knelt by his cot in the prison and prayed for his soul with as much confidence as I would kneel by your bedside. Oh! the Lord, long-suffering, merciful, and gracious; height above all height, depth below all depth, and any man who cries for mercy shall get it. But who would want to live a life hostile to the best interests of society, even though in his last moments he could make his peace with God and enter heaven? So I stand here before the young men, and I am going to have a plain talk with you, and I am going to offer you some safeguards. I shall not preach to you as a minister preaches to a formalistic congregation. I have no gown, or bands, or surplice; but I take you by both hands, my dear brother, and from what I know of life, and from what I know of God, and from what I know of the promises of Divine grace, I shall solemnly yet cheerfully address you. God gives me a great many young men here Sabbath by Sabbath, and it is my great ambition not only to reach heaven myself, but to take them all along with me. And I will, I will, God helping me.

The first safeguard of which I want to speak is a love of home. There are those who have no idea of the pleasures that concentrate around that word "home." Perhaps your early abode was shadowed with vice or poverty. Harsh words, and petulance, and scowling may have destroyed all the sanctity of that spot. Love, kindness, and self-sacrifice, which have built their altars in so many abodes, were strangers in your father's house. God pity you, young man; you never had a home. But a multitude in this audience can look back to a spot that they can never forget. It may have been a lowly roof, but you cannot think of it this morning without a dash of emotion. You have seen nothing on earth that so stirred your soul. A stranger passing along that place might see nothing remarkable about it; but oh! how much it means to you. Fresco on palace wall does not mean so much to you as those rough-hewn rafters. Parks and bowers and trees on fashionable watering-place or country-seat do not mean so much to you as that brook that ran in front of the plain farm-house, and singing under the weeping willows. The barred gateway swung open by porter in full dress, does not mean as much to you as that swing-gate, your sister on one side of it, and you on the other; she gone fitteen years ago into glory. That scene coming back to you to-day, as you swept backward and forward on the gate, singing the songs of your childhood. But there are those here who have their second dwelling-place. It is your adopted home. That also is sacred forever. There you established the first family altar. There your children were born. In that room flapped the wing of the death angel. Under that roof, when your work was done, you expect to lie down and die. There is only one word in all the language that can convey your idea of that place, and that word is "home." Now, let me say that I never knew a man who was faithful to his early and adopted home who was given over at the same time to any gross form of wickedness. If you find more enjoyment in the club-room, in the literary society, in the art-saloon, than you do in these unpretending home pleasures, you are on the road to ruin. Though you may be cut off from your early associates, and though you may be separated from all your kindred, young man, is there not a room somewhere that you can call your own? Though it be the fourth story of a third-class boarding house, into that room gather books, and pictures, and a harp. Hang your mother's portrait over the mantel. Bid unholy mirth stand back from that threshold. Consecrate some spot in that room with the knee of prayer. By the memory of other days, a father's counsel, a mother's love, and a sister's confidence, call it home.

Another safeguard for these young men is industrious habit. There are a great many people trying to make their way through the world with their wits instead of by honest toil. There is a young man who comes from the country to the city. He fails twice before he is as old as his father was when he first saw the spires of the great town. At twenty-one years of age he knows Wall Street from Trinity Church to East River docks. He is seated in his room at a rent of $2,000 a year, waiting for the banks to declare their dividends and the stocks to run up. After awhile he gets impatient. He tries to improve his penmanship by making copy-plates of other merchants' signatures! Never mind—all is right in business. After awhile he has his estate. Now is the time for him to retire to the country, amid the flocks and the herds, to culture the domestic virtues. Now the young men who were his schoolmates in boyhood will come, and with their ox teams draw him logs, and with their hard hands will help to heave up the castle. That is no fancy sketch; it is every-day life. I should not wonder if there were a rotten beam in that palace. I should not wonder if God should smite him with dire sicknesses, and pour into his cup a bitter draught that will thrill him with unbearable agony. I should not wonder if that man's children grew up to be to him a disgrace, and to make his life a shame. I should not wonder if that man died a dishonorable death, and were tumbled into a dishonorable grave, and then went into the gnashing of teeth. The way of the ungodly shall perish. Oh! young man, you must have industry of head, or hand, or foot, or perish. Do not have the idea that you can get along in the world by genius. The curse of this country to-day is genius—men with large self-conceit and nothing else. The man who proposes to make his living by his wits probably has not any. I should rather be an ox, plain, and plodding and useful, than to be an eagle, high-flying and good-for-nothing but to pick out the eyes of carcasses. Even in the Garden of Eden, it was not safe for Adam to be idle, so God made him an horticulturist; and if the married pair had kept busy dressing the vines, they would not have been sauntering under the trees, hankering after fruit that ruined them and their posterity! Proof positive of the fact that when people do not attend to their business they get into mischief. "Go to the ant, thou sluggard; consider her ways and be wise; which, having no overseer or guide, provideth her food in the summer and gathereth her meat in the harvest." Satan is a roaring lion, and you can never destroy him by gun or pistol or sword. The weapons with which you are to beat him back are hammer, and adze, and saw, and pickaxe, and yardstick, and the weapon of honest toil. Work, work, or die.

Another safeguard that I want to present to these young men is a high ideal of life. Sometimes soldiers going into battle shoot into the ground instead of into the hearts of their enemies. They are apt to take aim too low, and it is very often that the captain, going into conflict with his men, will cry out, "Now, men, aim high!" The fact is that in life a great many men take no aim at all. The artist plans out his entire thought before he puts it upon canvas, before he takes up the crayon or the chisel. An architect thinks out the entire building before the workmen begin. Although everything may seem to be unorganized, that architect has in his mind every Corinthian column, every Gothic arch, every Byzantine capital. A poet thinks out the entire plot of his poem before he begins to chime the cantos of tinkling rhythms. And yet there are a great many men who start the important structure of human life without knowing whether it is going to be a rude Tartar's hut or a St. Mark's Cathedral, and begin to write out the intricate poem of their life without knowing whether it is to be a Homer's "Odyssey" or a rhymester's botch. Out of one thousand, nine hundred and ninety-nine have no life-plot. Booted and spurred and caparisoned, they hasten along, and I run out and I say: "Hallo, man! Whither away?" "Nowhere!" they say. Oh! young man, make every day's duty a filling up of the great life-plot. Alas! that there should be on this sea of life so many ships that seem bound for no port. They are swept every whither by wind and wave, up by the mountains and down by the valleys. They sail with no chart. They gaze on no star. They long for no harbor. Oh! young man, have a high ideal and press to it, and it will be a mighty safeguard. There never were grander opportunities opening before young men than are opening now. Young men of the strong arm, and of the stout heart, and of the bounding step, I marshal you to-day for a great achievement.

Another safeguard is a respect for the Sabbath. Tell me how a young man spends his Sabbath, and I will tell you what are his prospects in business, and I will tell you what are his prospects for the eternal world. God has thrust into our busy life a sacred day when we are to look after our souls. Is it exorbitant, after giving six days to the feeding and the clothing of these perishable bodies, that God should demand one day for the feeding and the clothing of the immortal soul? Our bodies are seven-day clocks, and they need to be wound up, and if they are not wound up they run down into the grave. No man can continuously break the Sabbath and keep his physical and mental health. Ask those aged men and they will tell you they never knew men who continuously broke the Sabbath who did not fail either in mind, body or moral principle. A manufacturer gave this as his experience. He said: "I owned a factory on the Lehigh. Everything prospered. I kept the Sabbath, and everything went on well. But one Sabbath morning I bethought myself of a new shuttle, and I thought I would invent that shuttle before sunset; and I refused all food and drink until I had completed that shuttle. By sundown I had completed it. The next day, Monday, I showed to my workmen and friends this new shuttle. They all congratulated me on my great success. I put that shuttle into play. I enlarged my business; but, sir, that Sunday's work cost me $30,000. From that day everything went wrong. I failed in business, and I lost my mill." Oh, my friends, keep the Lord's day. You may think it old-fogy advice, but I give it to you now: "Remember the Sabbath day and keep it holy. Six days shalt thou labor and do all thy work; but the seventh is the Sabbath of the Lord thy God; in it thou shalt not do any work." A man said that he would prove that all this was a fallacy, and so he said: "I shall raise a Sunday crop." And he ploughed the field on the Sabbath, and then he put in the seed on the Sabbath and he cultured the ground on the Sabbath. When the harvest was ripe he reaped it on the Sabbath, and he carried it into the mow on the Sabbath, and then he stood out defiant to his Christian neighbors and said: "There, that is my Sunday crop, and it is all garnered." After awhile a storm came up, and a great darkness, and the lightnings of heaven struck the barn, and away went his Sunday crop!

There is one safeguard that I want to present. I have saved it until the last because I want it to be the more emphatic. The great safeguard for every young man is the Christian religion. Nothing can take the place of it. You may have gracefulness enough to put to the blush Lord Chesterfield, you may have foreign languages dropping from your tongue, you may discuss laws and literature, you may have a pen of unequaled polish and power, you may have so much business tact that you can get the largest salary in a banking house, you may be as sharp as Herod and as strong as Samson, and with as long locks as those which hung Absalom, and yet you have no safety against temptation. Some of you look forward to life with great despondency. I know it. I see it in your faces from time to time. You say: "All the occupations and professions are full, and there's no chance for me." "Oh! young man, cheer up, I will tell you how you can make your fortune. Seek first the kingdom of God and His righteousness, and all other things will be added. I know you do not want to be mean in this matter. You will not empty the brimming cup of life, and then pour the dregs on God's altar. To a generous Saviour you will not act like that; you have not the heart to act like that. That is not manly. That is not honorable. That is not brave. Your great want is a new heart, and in the name of the Lord Jesus Christ I tell you so to-day, and the blessed Spirit presses through the solemnities of this hour to put the cup of life to your thirsty lips. Oh! thrust it not back. Mercy presents it—bleeding mercy, long-suffering Mercy. Despise all other friendships, prove recreant to all other bargains, but despise God's love for your dying soul—do not do that. There comes a crisis in a man's life, and the trouble is he does not know it is the crisis. I got a letter this week I thought to have brought it with me to church and read you a portion of it—in which a man says to me:

"I start out now to preach the gospel of righteousness and temperance to the people. Do you remember me? I am the man who appeared at the close of the service when you were worshipping in the chapel after you came from Philadelphia. Do you remember at the close of the service a man coming up to you all a tremble with conviction, and crying out for mercy, and telling you he had a very bad business, and he thought he would change it? That was the turning point in my history. I gave up my bad business. I gave my heart to God, and the desire to serve Him has grown upon me all these years, until now woe is unto me if I preach not the Gospel."

That Sunday night, in the chapel, now the Lay College, was the turning point in that young man's history. This very Sabbath hour will be the turning point in the history of a hundred young men in this house. God help us. I once stood on an anniversary platform with a clergyman who told this marvelous story. He said:

"Thirty years ago two young men started out to attend Park Theater, New York, to see a play which made religion ridiculous and hypocritical. They had been brought up in Christian families. They started for the theater to see that vile play, and their early convictions came back upon them. They felt it was not right to go, but still they went. They came to the door of the theater. One of the young men stopped and started for home, but returned and came up to the door, but had not the courage to go in. He again started for home, and went home. The other young man went in. He went from one degree of temptation to another. Caught in the whirl of frivolity and sin, he sank lower and lower. He lost his business position. He lost his morals. He lost his soul. He died a dreadful death, not one star of mercy shining on it. I stand before you to-day," said that minister, "to thank God that for twenty years I have been permitted to preach the Gospel. I am the other young man."

Oh! you see that was the turning point—the one went back, the other went on. That great roaring world of New York life will soon break in upon you, young men. Will the wild wave dash out the impressions of this day as an ocean billow dashes letters out of the sand on the beach? You need something better than this world can give you. I beat on your heart and it sounds hollow. You want something great and grand and glorious to fill it, and here is the religion that can do it. God save you!

CHAPTER XVI.

THE VOICES OF THE STREET.

Wisdom crieth without, she uttereth her voice in the streets. —Prov. i: 20.

We are all ready to listen to the voices of nature—the voices of the mountain, the voices of the sea, the voices of the storm, the voices of the star. As in some of the cathedrals in Europe, there is an organ at either end of the building, and the one instrument responds musically to the other, so in the great cathedral of nature, day responds to day, and night to night, and flower to flower, and star to star, in the great harmonies of the universe. The spring time is an evangelist in blossoms preaching of God's love; and the winter is a prophet—white bearded—denouncing woe against our sins. We are all ready to listen to the voices of nature; but how few of us learn anything from the voices of the noisy and dusty street. You go to your mechanism, and to your work, and to your merchandise, and you come back again—and often with how different a heart you pass through the streets. Are there no things for us to learn from these pavements over which we pass? Are there no tufts of truth growing up between these cobblestones? beaten with the feet of toil, and pain, and pleasure, the slow tread of old age, and the quick step of childhood? Aye, there are great harvests to be reaped; and this morning I thrust in the sickle because the harvest is ripe. "Wisdom crieth without, she uttereth her voice in the streets."

In the first place, the street impresses me with the fact that *this life is a scene of toil and struggle.* By ten o'clock every day the city is jarring with wheels, and shuffling with feet, and humming with voices, and covered with the breath of smoke-stacks, and a-rush with traffickers. Once in awhile you find a man going along with folded arms and with leisure step, as though he had nothing to do; but for the most part, as you find men going down these streets on the way to business, there is anxiety in their faces, as though they had some errand which must be executed at the first possible moment. You are jostled by those who have bargains to make and notes to sell. Up this ladder with a hod of bricks, out of this bank with a roll of bills, on this dray with a load of goods, digging a cellar, or shingling a roof, or shoeing a horse, or building a wall, or mending a watch, or binding a book. Industry, with her thousand arms and thousand eyes, and thousand feet, goes on singing her song of work! work! work! while the mills drum it, and the steam-whistles fife it. All this is not because men love toil. Some one remarked: "Every man is as lazy as he can afford to be." But it is because necessity with stern brow and with uplifted whip, stands over you ready whenever you relax your toil to make your shoulders sting with the lash. Can it be that passing up and down these streets on your way to work and business that you do not learn anything of the world's toil, and anxiety, and struggle? Oh! how many drooping hearts, how many eyes on the watch, how many miles traveled, how many burdens carried, how many losses suffered, how many battles fought, how many victories gained, how many defeats suffered, how many exasperations endured—what losses, what hunger, what wretchedness, what pallor, what disease, what agony, what despair!

Sometimes I have stopped at the corner of the street as the multitudes went hither and yon, and it has seemed to be a great pantomine, and as I looked upon it my heart broke. This great tide of human life that goes down the street is a rapid, tossed, and turned aside, and dashed ahead, and driven back—beautiful in its confusion, and confused in its beauty. In the carpeted aisles of the forest, in the woods from which the eternal shadow is never lifted, on the shore of the sea over whose iron coast tosses the tangled foam sprinkling the cracked cliffs with a baptism of whirlwind and tempest, is the best place to study God; but in the rushing, swarming, raving street is the best place to study man. Going down to your place of business and coming home again, I charge you look about—see these signs of poverty, of wretchedness, of hunger, of sin, of bereavement—and as you go through the streets, and come back through the streets, gather up in the arms of your prayer all the sorrow, all the losses, all the suffering, all the bereavements of those whom you pass, and present them in prayer before an all-sympathetic God. In the great day of eternity there will be thousands of persons with whom you in this world never exchanged one word, will rise up and call you blessed; and there will be a thousand fingers pointed at you in heaven, saying: "That is the man, that is the woman, who helped me when I was hungry, and sick, and wandering, and lost, and heart-broken. That is the man, that is the woman," and the blessing will come down upon you as Christ shall say: "I was hungry and ye fed me, I was naked and ye clothed me, I was sick and in prison and ye visited me; inasmuch as ye did it to these poor waifs of the streets, ye did it to Me."

Again, the street impresses me with the fact that *all*

classes and conditions of society must commingle. We sometimes culture a wicked exclusiveness. Intellect despises ignorance. Refinement will have nothing to do with boorishness. Gloves hate the sunburned hand, and the high forehead despises the flat head; and the trim hedgerow will have nothing to do with the wild corpse-wood, and the Athens hates Nazareth. This ought not to be so. The astronomer must come down from his starry revelry and help us in our navigation. The surgeon must come away from his study of the human organism and set our broken bones. The chemist must come away from his laboratory, where he has been studying analysis and synthesis, and help us to understand the nature of the soils. I bless God that all classes of people are compelled to meet on the street. The glittering coach-wheel clashes against the scavenger's cart. Fine robes run against the pedlar's pack. Robust health meets wan sickness. Honesty confronts fraud. Every class of people meets every other class. Independence and modesty, pride and humility, purity and beastliness, frankness and hypocrisy, meeting on the same block, in the same street, in the same city. Oh! that is what Solomon meant when he said: "The rich and the poor meet together; the Lord is the Maker of them all." I like this democratic principle of the Gospel of Jesus Christ which recognizes the fact that we stand before God on one and the same platform. Do not take on any airs; whatever position you have gained in society, you are nothing but a man, born of the same parent, regenerated by the same Spirit, cleansed in the same blood, to lie down in the same dust, to get up in the same resurrection. It is high time that we all acknowledged not only the Fatherhood of God, but the brotherhood of man.

Again, the street impresses me with the fact that *it is*

a very hard thing for a man to keep his heart right and to get to heaven. Infinite temptations spring upon us from these places of public concourse. Amid so much affluence how much temptation to covetousness, and to be discontented with our humble lot. Amid so many opportunities for over-reaching, what temptation to extortion. Amid so much display, what temptation to vanity. Amid so many saloons of strong drink, what allurement to dissipation. In the maelstroms and hell gates of the street, how many make quick and eternal shipwreck. If a man-of-war comes back from a battle, and is towed into the navy-yard, we go down to look at the splintered spars and count the bullet-holes, and look with patriotic admiration on the flag that floated in victory from the masthead. But that man is more of a curiosity who has gone through thirty years of the sharp-shooting of business life, and yet sails on, victor over the temptations of the street. Oh! how many have gone down under the pressure, leaving not so much as the patch of canvas to tell where they perished. They never had any peace. Their dishonesties kept tolling in their ears. If I had an axe, and could split open the beams of that fine house, perhaps I would find in the very heart of it a skeleton. In his very best wine there is a smack of poor man's sweat. Oh! is it strange that when a man has devoured widows' houses, he is disturbed with indigestion? All the forces of nature are against him. The floods are ready to drown him, and the earthquake to swallow him, and the fires to consume him, and the lightnings to smite him. Aye, all the armies of God are on the street, and in the day when the crowns of heaven are distributed, some of the brightest of them will be given to those men who were faithful to God and faithful to the souls of others amid the marts of business, proving themselves the heroes of the street. Mighty were their temptations, mighty was their deliverance, and mighty shall be their triumph.

Again, the street impresses me with the fact that *life is full of pretension and sham.* What subterfuge, what double dealing, what two-facedness. Do all people who wish you good morning really hope for you a happy day? Do all the people who shake hands love each other? Are all those anxious about your health who inquire concerning it? Do all want to see you who ask you to call? Does all the world know half as much as it pretends to know? Is there not many a wretched stock of goods with a brilliant store window? Passing up and down these streets to your business and your work, are you not impressed with the fact that society is hollow, and that there are subterfuges and pretensions? Oh! how many there are who swagger and strut, and how few people who are natural and walk. While fops simper, and fools chuckle, and simpletons giggle, how few people are natural and laugh. The courtesan and the libertine go down the street in beautiful apparel, while within the heart there are volcanoes of passion consuming their life away. I say these things not to create in you incredulity or misanthropy, nor do I forget there are thousands of people a great deal better than they seem; but I do not think any man so prepared for the conflict of this life until he knows this particular peril. Ehud comes pretending to pay his tax to king Eglon, and while he stands in front of the king, stabs him through with a dagger until the haft went in after the blade. Judas Iscariot kissed Christ.

Again, the street impresses me with the fact that it is *a great field for Christian charity.* There are hunger and suffering, and want and wretchedness, in the country; but these evils chiefly congregate in our great cities. On every street crime prowls, and drunkenness staggers, and shame winks, and pauperism thrusts out its hand asking for alms. Here, want is most squalid and hunger is most lean. A Christian man, going along a street in New York, saw a poor lad, and he stopped and said: "My boy, do you know how to read and write?" The boy made no answer. The man asked the question twice and thrice. "Can you read and write?" and then the boy answered, with a tear plashing on the back of his hand. He said in defiance: "No, sir; I can't read nor write, neither. God, sir, don't want me to read and write. Didn't he take away my father so long ago I never remember to have seen him? and havn't I had to go along the streets to get something to fetch home to eat for the folks? and didn't I, as soon as I could carry a basket, have to go out and pick up cinders, and never have no schooling, sir? God don't want me to read, sir. I can't read, nor write neither." Oh, these poor wanderers? They have no chance. Born in degradation, as they get up from their hands and knees to walk, they take their first step on the road to despair. Let us go forth in the name of the Lord Jesus Christ to rescue them. Let us ministers not be afraid of soiling our black clothes while we go down on that mission. While we are tying an elaborate knot in our cravat, or while we are in the study rounding off some period rhetorically, we might be saving a soul from death, and hiding a multitude of sins. O Christian laymen, go out on this work. If you are not willing to go forth yourself, then give of your means; and if you are too lazy to go, and if you are too stingy to help, then get out of the way, and hide yourself in the dens and caves of the earth, lest, when Christ's chariot comes along, the horses' hoofs trample you into the mire. Beware lest the thousands of the destitute of your city, in the last great day, rise up and curse your stupidity and your neglect. Down to work! Lift them up! One cold winter's day, as a Christian man was going along the Battery in New York, he saw a little girl seated at the gate, shivering in the cold. He said to her: "My child, what do you sit there for, this cold day?" "Oh," she replied, "I am waiting—I am waiting for somebody to come and take care of me." "Why?" said the man, "what makes you think anybody will come and take care of you?" "Oh," she said, my mother died last week, and I was crying very much, and she said: 'Don't cry, my dear; though I am gone and your father is gone, the Lord will send somebody to take care of you.' My mother never told a lie; she said some one would come and take care of me, and I am waiting for them to come." O yes, they are waiting for you. Men who have money, men who have influence, men of churches, men of great hearts, gather them in, gather them in. It is not the will of your Heavenly Father that one of these little ones should perish.

Lastly, the street impresses me with the fact that *all the people are looking forward*. I see expectancy written on almost every face I meet between here and Fulton ferry, or walking the whole length of Broadway. Where you find a thousand people walking straight on, you only find one man stopping and looking back. The fact is, God made us all to look ahead, because we are immortal. In this tramp of the multitude on the streets, I hear the tramp of a great host, marching and marching for eternity. Beyond the office, the store, the shop, the street, there is a world, populous and tremendous. Through God's grace, may you reach that blessed place. A great throng fills those boulevards and the streets are arush with the chariots of conquerors. The inhabitants go up and down, but they never weep and they never toil. A river flows through that city, with rounded and luxurious banks, and trees of life laden with everlasting fruitage bend their branches to dip the crystal. No plumed hearse rattles over that pavement, for they are never sick. With immortal health glowing in every vein they know not how to die. Those towers of strength, those palaces of beauty, gleam in the light of a sun that never sets. Oh, heaven, beautiful heaven! Heaven, where our friends are. They take no census in that city, for it is inhabited by "a multitude which no man can number." Rank above rank. Host above host. Gallery above gallery, sweeping all around the heavens. Thousands of thousands. Millions of millions. Quadrillions of quadrillions. Quintillions of quintillions. Blessed are they who enter in through the gate into that city. Oh! start for it this morning. Through the blood of the great sacrifice of the Son of God, take up your march for heaven. The spirit and the bride say come, and whosoever will, let him come and take of the water of life "freely." Join this great throng who this morning, for the first time, espouse their faith in Christ. All the doors of invitation are open. "And I saw twelve gates and they were twelve pearls."

CHAPTER XVII.

HEROES IN COMMON LIFE.

Thou, therefore, endure hardness.—II. Timothy ii: 3.

Historians are not slow to acknowledge the merits of great military chieftains. We have the full-length portraits of the Cromwells, the Washingtons, the Napoleons, and the Wellingtons of the world. History is not written in black ink, but with red ink of human blood. The gods of human ambition do not drink from bowls made out of silver, or gold, or precious stones, but out of the bleached skulls of the fallen. But I am now to unroll before you a scroll of heroes that the world has never acknowledged; those who faced no guns, blew no bugle-blast, conquered no cities, chained no captives to their chariot-wheels, and yet, in the great day of eternity, will stand higher than those whose names startled the nations; and seraph, and rapt spirit, and archangel will tell their deeds to a listening universe. I mean the heroes of common, every-day life.

In this roll, in the first place, I find all the heroes of the sick room. When Satan had failed to overcome Job, he said to God, "Put forth thy hand and touch his bones and his flesh, and he will curse thee to thy face." Satan had found out what we have all found out, that sickness is the greatest test of one's character. A man who can stand that can stand anything. To be shut in a room as fast as though it were a bastile. To be so nervous you cannot endure the tap of a child's foot. To have luxuriant fruit, which tempts the appetite of the robust and healthy, excite our loathing and disgust when it first appears on the platter. To have the rapier of pain strike through the side, or across the temples, like a razor, or to put the foot into a vice, or throw the whole body into a blaze of fever. Yet there have been men and women, but more women than men, who have cheerfully endured this hardness. Through years of exhausting rheumatisms and excruciating neuralgias they have gone, and through bodily distresses that rasped the nerves, and tore the muscles, and paled the cheeks, and stooped the shoulders. By the dim light of the sick room taper they saw on their wall the picture of that land where the inhabitants are never sick. Through the dead silence of the night they heard the chorus of the angels. The cancer ate away her life from week to week and day to day, and she became weaker and weaker, and every "good night" was feebler than the "good night" before—yet never sad. The children looked up into her face and saw suffering transformed into a heavenly smile. Those who suffered on the battle-field, amid shot and shell, were not so much heroes and heroines as those who in the field hospital and in the asylum had fevers which no ice could cool and no surgery could cure. No shout of comrade to cheer them, but numbness, and aching, and homesickness—yet willing to suffer, confident in God, hopeful of heaven. Heroes of rheumatism. Heroes of neuralgia. Heroes of spinal complaint. Heroes of sick headache. Heroes of lifelong invalidism. Heroes and heroines. They shall reign for ever and for ever.

Hark! I catch just one note of the eternal anthem: "There shall be no more pain." Bless God for that.

In this roll I also find the heroes of toil, who do their work uncomplainingly. It is comparatively easy to lead a regiment into battle when you know that the whole nation will applaud the victory; it is comparatively easy to doctor the sick when you know that your skill will be appreciated by a large company of friends and relatives; it is comparatively easy to address an audience when in the gleaming eyes and the flushed cheeks you know that your sentiments are adopted; but to do sewing where you expect that the employer will come and thrust his thumb through the work to show how imperfect it is, or to have the whole garment thrown back on you to be done over again; to build a wall and know there will be no one to say you did it well, but only a swearing employer howling across the scaffold; to work until your eyes are dim and your back aches, and your heart faints, and to know that if you stop before night your children will starve. Ah! the sword has not slain so many as the needle. The great battle-fields of our last war were not Gettysburg and Shiloh and South Mountain. The great battle-fields of the last war were in the arsenals, and in the shops and in the attics, where women made army jackets for a sixpence. They toiled on until they died. They had no funeral eulogium, but in the name of my God, this morning, I enroll their names among those of whom the world was not worthy. Heroes of the needle. Heroes of the sewing-machine. Heroes of the attic. Heroes of the cellar. Heroes and heroines. Bless God for them.

In this roll I also find the heroes who have uncomplainingly endured domestic injustices. There are men who for their toil and anxiety have no sympathy in their homes. Exhausting application to business gets them a livelihood, but an unfrugal wife scatters it. He is fretted at from the moment he enters the door until he comes out of it. The exasperations of business life augmented by the exasperations of domestic life. Such men are laughed at, but they have a heart-breaking trouble, and they would have long ago gone into appalling dissipations but for the grace of God. Society to-day is strewn with the wrecks of men who under the north-east storm of domestic infelicity have been driven on the rocks. There are tens of thousands of drunkards in this country to-day, made such by their wives. That is not poetry! That is prose! But the wrong is generally in the opposite direction. You would not have to go far to find a wife whose life is a perpetual martyrdom. Something heavier than a stroke of the fist; unkind words, staggerings home at midnight, and constant maltreatment, which have left her only a wreck of what she was on that day when in the midst of a brilliant assemblage the vows were taken, and full organ played the wedding march, and the carriage rolled away with the benediction of the people. What was the burning of Latimer and Ridley at the stake compared with this? Those men soon became unconscious in the fire, but here is a fifty years' martyrdom, a fifty years' putting to death, yet uncomplaining. No bitter words when the rollicking companions at two o'clock in the morning pitch the husband dead drunk into the front entry. No bitter words when wiping from the swollen brow the blood struck out in a midnight carousal. Bending over the battered and bruised form of him who, when he took her from her father's home, promised love, and kindness, and protection, yet nothing but sympathy, and prayers, and forgiveness before they are asked for. No bitter words when the family Bible goes for rum, and the pawnbroker's shop gets the last decent dress. Some day, desiring to evoke the story of her sorrows, you say: "Well, how are you getting along now?" and rallying her trembling voice, and quieting her quivering lip, she says: "Pretty well, I thank you, pretty well." She never will tell you. In the delirium of her last sickness she may tell all the secrets of her lifetime, but she will not tell that. Not until the books of eternity are opened on the thrones of judgment will ever be known what she has suffered. Oh! ye who are twisting a garland for the victor, put it on that pale brow. When she is dead the neighbors will beg linen to make her a shroud, and she will be carried out in a plain box with no silver plate to tell her years, for she has lived a thousand years of trial and anguish. The gamblers and swindlers who destroyed her husband will not come to the funeral. One carriage will be enough for that funeral—one carriage to carry the orphans and the two Christian women who presided over the obsequies. But there is a flash, and the opening of a celestial door, and a shout: "Lift up your head, ye everlasting gate, and let her come in!" And Christ will step forth and say: "Come in! ye suffered with me on earth, be glorified with me in heaven." What is the highest throne in heaven? You say: "The throne of the Lord God Almighty and the Lamb." No doubt about it. What is the next highest throne in heaven? While I speak it seems to me that it will be the throne of the drunkard's wife, if she, with cheerful patience, endured all her earthly torture. Heroes and heroines.

I find also in this roll the heroes of Christian charity. We all admire the George Peabodys and the James Lenoxes of the earth, who give tens and hundreds of thousands of dollars to good objects. A few days ago Moses H. Grinnell was buried, and the most significant thing about the ceremonies, as I read them, was that there was no sermon and no oration; a plain hymn, a prayer, and a benediction. Well, I said, that is very beautiful. All Christendom pronounces the eulogium of Moses H. Grinnell, and the icebergs that stand as monuments to Franklin and his men will stand as the monuments of this great merchant, and the sunlight that plays upon the glittering cliff will write his epitaph. But I am speaking this morning of those who, out of their pinched poverty, help others—of such men as those Christian missionaries at the West, who are living on $250 a year that they may proclaim Christ to the people, one of them, writing to the secretary in New York, saying: "I thank you for that $25. Until yesterday we have had no meat in our house for three months. We have suffered terribly. My children have no shoes this winter." And of those people who have only a half loaf of bread, but give a piece of it to others who are hungrier; and of those who have only a scuttle of coal, but help others to fuel; and of those who have only a dollar in their pocket, and give twenty-five cents to somebody else; and of that father who wears a shabby coat, and of that mother who wears a faded dress, that their children may be well apparelled. You call them paupers, or ragmuffins, or emigrants. I call them heroes and heroines. You and I may not know where they live, or what their name is. God knows, and they have more angels hovering over them than you and I have, and they will have a higher seat in heaven.

They may have only a cup of cold water to give a poor traveler, or may have only picked a splinter from under the nail of a child's finger, or have put only two mites into the treasury, but the Lord knows them. Considering what they had, they did more than we have ever done, and their faded dress will become a white robe, and the small room will be an eternal mansion, and the old hat will be a coronet of victory, and all the applause of earth and all the shouting of heaven will be drowned out when God rises up to give his reward to those humble workers in his kingdom, and to say to them: "Well done, good and faithful servant." You have all seen or heard of the ruin of Melrose Abbey. I suppose in some respects it is the most exquisite ruin on earth. And yet, looking at it I was not so impressed—you may set it down to bad taste—but I was not so deeply stirred as I was at a tombstone at the foot of that abbey—the tombstone placed by Walter Scott over the grave of an old man who had served him for a good many years in his house—the inscription most significant, but I defy any man to stand there and read it without tears coming into his eyes—the epitaph: "Well done, good and faithful servent." Oh! when our work is over, will it be found that because of anything, we have done for God, or the church, or suffering humanity, that such an inscription is appropriate for us? God grant it.

Who are those who were bravest and deserved the greatest monument—Lord Claverhouse and his burly soldiers or John Brown, the Edinburgh carrier and his wife? Mr. Atkins, the persecuted minister of Jesus Christ in Scotland, was secreted by John Brown and his wife, and Claverhouse rode up one day with his armed men and shouted in front of the house. John Brown's little girl came out. He said to her: "Well, miss, is Mr. Atkins here?" She made no answer, for she could not betray the minister of the Gospel. "Ha!" Claverhouse said, "then you are a chip of the old block, are you? I have something in my pocket for you. It is a nosegay. Some people call it a thumbscrew, but I call it a nosegay." And he got off his horse, and he put it on the little girl's hand, and begin to turn it until the bones cracked, and she cried. He said, "don't cry, don't cry; this isn't a thumbscrew; this is a nosegay." And they heard the child's cry, and the father and mother came out, and Claverhouse said, "Ha! it seems that you three have laid your holy heads together determined to die like all the rest of your hypocritical, canting, snivelling crew; rather than give up good Mr. Atkins, pious Mr. Atkins, you would die. I have a telescope with me that will improve your vision," and he pulled out a pistol. "Now," he said, "you old pragmatical, lest you should catch cold in this cold morning of Scotland, and for the honor and safety of the king, to say nothing of the glory of God and the good of our souls, I will proceed simply and in the neatest and most expeditious style possible to blow your brains out." John Brown fell upon his knees and began to pray. "Ah!" said Claverhouse, "look out, if you are going to pray; steer clear of the king, the council, and Richard Cameron." "O! Lord," said John Brown, "since it seems to be thy will that I should leave this world for a world where I can love thee better and serve thee more, I put this poor widow woman and these helpless, fatherless children into thy hands. We have been together in peace a good while, but now we must look forth to a better meeting in heaven, and as for these poor creatures, blindfolded and infatuated, that stand before me, convert them before it be too late, and may they who have sat in judgment in this lonely place on this blessed morning, upon me, a poor, defenceless fellow-creature—may they, in the last judgment find that mercy which they have refused to me, thy most unworthy, but faithful servant. Amen." He rose up and said, "Isabel, the hour has come of which I spoke to you on the morning when I proposed hand and heart to you; and are you willing now, for the love of God, to let me die?" She put her arms around him and said:—"The

Lord gave, and the Lord hath taken away. Blessed be the name of the Lord!" "Stop that snivelling," said Claverhouse. "I have had enough of it. Soldiers, do your work. Take aim! Fire!" and the head of John Brown was scattered on the ground. While the wife was gathering up in her apron the fragments of her husband's head—gathering them up for burial—Claverhouse looked into her face and said, "Now, my good woman, how do you feel now about your bonnie man?" "Oh!" she said, "I always thought weel of him; he has been very good to me; I had no reason for thinking anything but weel of him, and I think better of him now." Oh! what a grand thing it will be in the last day to see God pick out his heroes and heroines. Who are those paupers of eternity trudging off from the gates of heaven? Who are they? The Lord Claverhouses and the Herods and those who had sceptres, and crowns, and thrones, but they lived for their own aggrandisement, and they broke the heart of nations. Heroes of earth, but paupers in eternity. I beat the drums of their eternal despair. Woe! woe! woe!

But there is great excitement in heaven. Why those long processions? Why the booming of that great bell in the tower? It is coronation day in heaven.

Who are those rising on the thrones, with crowns of eternal royalty? They must have been great people on earth, world-renowned people. No. They taught in a ragged school. Taught in a ragged school! Is that all? That is all. Who are those souls waving sceptres of eternal dominion? Why, they were little children who waited on invalid mothers. That all? That is all. She was called "Little Mary" on earth. She is an empress now. Who are that great multitude on the highest thrones of heaven? Who are they? Why, they fed the hungry, they clothed the naked, they healed the sick, they comforted the heart-broken. They never found any rest until they put their head down on the pillow of the sepulchre. God watched them. God laughed defiance at the enemies who put their heels hard down on these His dear children; and one day the Lord struck His hand so hard on His thigh that the omnipotent sword rattled in the buckler, as He said: "I am their God, and no weapon formed against them shall prosper." What harm can the world do you when the Lord Almighty with unsheathed sword fights for you."

I preach this sermon this morning in comfort. Go home to the place just where God has put you to play the hero or the heroine. Do not envy any man his money, or his applause, or his social position. Do not envy any woman her wardrobe, or her exquisite appearance. Be the hero or the heroine. If there be no flour in the house, and you do not know where your children are to get bread, listen, and you will hear something tapping against the window-pane. Go to the window and you will find it is the beak of a raven, and open the window, and there will fly in the messenger that fed Elijah. Do you think that the God who grows the cotton of the South will let you freeze for lack of clothes? Do you think that the God who allowed the disciples on Sunday morning to go into the grain-field, and then take the grain and rub it in their hands and eat—do you think God will let you starve? Did you ever hear the experience of that old man: "I have been young, and now am I old, yet have I never seen the righteous forsaken, or his seed begging bread?" Get up out of your discouragement, O! troubled soul, O! sewing woman, O! man, kicked and cuffed by unjust employers, O! ye who are hard beset in the battle of life and know not which way to turn, O! you bereft one, O! you sick one with complaints you have told to no one, come and get the comfort of this subject. Listen to our great Captain's cheer: "To him that overcometh will I give to eat of the fruit of the tree of life which is in the midst of the Paradise of God."

CHAPTER XVIII.

THE MIDNIGHT HORSEMAN.

Then I went up in the night by the brook and viewed the wall, and turned back, and entered by the gate of the valley, and so returned.—Nehemiah ii: 15.

A dead city is more suggestive than a living city—past Rome than present Rome—ruins rather than newly frescoed cathedral. But the best time to visit a ruin is by moonlight. The Coliseum is far more fascinating to the traveler after sundown than before. You may stand by daylight amid the monastic ruins of Melrose Abbey, and study shafted oriel, and rosetted stone and mullion, but they throw their strongest witchery by moonlight. Some of you remember what the enchanter of Scotland said in the "Lay of the Last Minstrel;"

"Wouldst thou view fair Melrose aright,
Go visit it by the pale moonlight."

Washington Irving describes the Andalusian moonlight upon the Alhambra ruins as amounting to an enchantment. My text presents you Jerusalem in ruins. The tower down. The gates down. The walls down. Everything down. Nehemiah on horseback, by moonlight looking upon the ruins. While he rides, there are some friends on foot going with him, for they do not want the many horses to disturb the suspicions of the people. These people do not know the secret of Nehemiah's heart, but they are going as a sort of body-guard.

I hear the clicking hoofs of the horse on which Nehemiah rides, as he guides it this way and that, into this gate and out of that, winding through that gate amid the *debris* of once great Jerusalem. Now the horse comes to a dead halt at the tumbled masonry where he cannot pass. Now he shies off at the charred timbers. Now he comes along where the water under the moonlight flashes from the mouth of the brazen dragon after which the gate was named. Heavy-hearted Nehemiah! Riding in and out, now by his old home desolated, now by the defaced Temple, now amid the scars of the city that had gone down under battering-ram and conflagration. The escorting party knows not what Nehemiah means. Is he getting crazy? Have his own personal sorrows, added to the sorrows of the nation, unbalanced his intellect? Still the midnight exploration goes on. Nehemiah on horseback rides through the fish gate, by the tower of the furnaces, by the king's pool, by the dragon well, in and out, in and out, until the midnight ride is completed, and Nehemiah dismounts from his horse, and to the amazed and confounded and incredulous body-guard, declares the dead secret of his heart when he says: "Come, now, let us build Jerusalem." "What, Nehemiah, have you any money?" "No." "Have you any kingly authority?" "No." "Have you any eloquence?" "No." Yet that midnight, moonlight ride of Nehemiah resulted in the glorious rebuilding of the city of Jerusalem. The people knew not how the thing was to be done, but with great enthusiasm they cried out: "Let us rise up now and build the city." Some people laughed and said it could not be done. Some people were infuriate and offered physical violence, saying the thing should not be done. But the workmen went right on, standing on the wall, trowel in one hand, sword in the other, until the work was gloriously completed. At that very time, in Greece, Xenophon was writing a history, and Plato was making philosophy, and Demosthenes was rattling his rhetorical thunder; but all of them together did not do so much for the world as this midnight, moonlight ride of praying, courageous, homesick, close-mouthed Nehemiah.

My subject first impresses me with the idea what an intense thing is church affection. Seize the bridle of that horse and stop Nehemiah. Why are you risking your life here in the night? Your horse will stumble over these ruins and fall on you. Stop this useless exposure of your life. No; Nehemiah will not stop. He at last tells us the whole story. He lets us know he was an exile in a far distant land, and he was a servant, a cup-bearer in the palace of Artaxerxes Longimanus, and one day, while he was handing the cup of wine to the king, the king said to him, "What is the matter with you? You are not sick. I know you must have some great trouble. What is the matter with you?" Then he told the king how that beloved Jerusalem was broken down; how that his father's tomb had been desecrated; how that the Temple had been dishonored and defaced; how that the walls were scattered and broken. "Well," says King Artaxerxes, "what do you want?" "Well," said the cup-bearer Nehemiah, "I want to go home. I want to fix up the grave of my father. I want to restore the beauty of the Temple. I want to rebuild the masonry of the city wall. Besides, I want passports so that I shall not be hindered in my journey. And besides that," as you will find in the context, "I want an order on the man who keeps your forest for just so much timber as I may need for the rebuilding of the city." "How long shall you be gone?" said the king. The time of absence is arranged. In hot haste this seeming adventurer comes to Jerusalem, and in my text we find him on horseback, in the midnight, riding around the ruins. It is through the spectacles of this scene that we discover the ardent attachment of Nehemiah for sacred Jerusalem, which in all ages has been the type of the church of God, our Jerusalem, which we love just as much as Nehemiah loved his Jerusalem. The fact is that you love the church of God so much that there is no spot on earth so sacred, unless it be your own fireside. The church has been to you so much comfort and illumination that there is nothing that makes you so irate as to have it talked against. If there have been times when you have been carried into captivity by sickness, you longed for the Church, our holy Jerusalem, just as much as Nehemiah longed for his Jerusalem, and the first day you came out you came to the house of the Lord. When the temple was in ruins, as ours was five years ago, like Nehemiah, you walked around and looked at it, and in the moonlight you stood listening if you could not hear the voice of the dead organ, the psalm of the expired Sabbaths. What Jerusalem was to Nehemiah, the Church of God is to you. Sceptics and infidels may scoff at the Church as an obsolete affair, as a relic of the dark ages, as a convention of goody-goody people, but all the impression they have ever made on your mind against the Church of God is absolutely nothing. You would make more sacrifices for it to-day than for any other institution, and if it were needful you would die in its defence. You can take the words of the kingly poet as he said: "If I forget thee, O Jerusalem, let my right hand forget her cunning." You understand in your own experience the pathos, the home-sickness, the courage, the holy enthusiasm of Nehemiah in his midnight moonlight ride around the ruins of his beloved Jerusalem.

Again, my text impresses me with the fact that, before reconstruction, there must be an exploration of ruins. Why was not Nehemiah asleep under the covers? Why was not his horse stabled in the midnight? Let the police of the city arrest this midnight rider, out on some mischief. No. Nehemiah is going to rebuild the city, and he is making the preliminary exploration. In this gate, out that gate, east, west, north, south. All through the ruins. The ruins must be explored before the work of reconstruction can begin. The reason that so many people in this day, apparently converted, do not stay converted is because they did not first explore the ruins of their own heart. The reason that there are so many professed Christians who in this day lie and forge and steal, and commit adultery, and go to the penitentiary, is because they first do not learn the ruin of their own heart. They have not found out that "the heart is deceitful above all things, and desperately wicked." They had an idea that they were almost right, and they built religion as a sort of extension, as an ornamental cupola. There was a superstructure of religion built on a substratum of unrepented sins. The trouble with a good deal of modern theology is that instead of building on the right foundation, it builds on the *debris* of an unreregenerated nature. They attempt to rebuild Jerusalem before, in the midnight of conviction, they have seen the ghastliness of the ruin. They have such a poor foundation for their religion that the first north-east storm of temptation blows them down. I have no faith in a man's conversion if he is not converted in the old-fashioned way—John Bunyan's way, John Wesley's way, John Calvin's way, Paul's way, Christ's way, God's way,

A dentist said to me a few days ago, "Does that hurt?" Said I, "Of course it hurts. It is in your business as in my profession. We have to hurt before we can help." You will never understand redemption until you understand ruin. A man tells me that some one is a member of the church. It makes no impression on my mind at all. I simply want to know whether he was converted in the old-fashioned way, or whether he was converted in the new-fashioned way. If he was converted in the old-fashioned way he will stand. If he was converted in the new-fashioned way he will not stand. That is all there is about it. A man comes to me to talk about religion. The first question I ask him is, "Do you feel yourself to be a sinner?" If he say, "Well, I--yes," the hesitancy makes me feel that that man wants a ride on Nehemiah's horse by midnight through the ruins—in by the gate of his affections, out by the gate of his will; and before he has got through with that midnight ride he will drop the reins on the horse's neck, and will take his right hand and smite on his heart and say, "God be merciful to me a sinner;" and before he has stabled his horse he will take his feet out of the stirrups, and he will slide down on the ground, and he will kneel, crying, "Have mercy on me, O God, according to thy loving-kindness, according unto the multitude of thy tender mercies; blot out my transgressions, for I acknowledge my transgressions, and my sins are ever before thee." Ah, my friends, you see this is not a complimentary gospel. That is what makes some people so mad. It comes to a man of a million dollars, and impenitent in his sins, and says, "You're a pauper." It comes to a woman of fairest cheek, who has never repented, and says, "You're a sinner." It comes to a man priding himself on his independence, and says, "You're bound hand and foot by the devil." It comes to our entire race and says, "You're a ruin, a ghastly ruin, an illimitable ruin." Satan sometimes says to me, "Why do you preach that truth? Why don't you preach a gospel with no repentance in it? Why don't you flatter men's hearts so that you make them feel all right? Why don't you preach a humanitarian gospel with no repentance in it, saying nothing about the ruin, talking all the time about redemption? Instead of preaching to five thousand you might preach to twenty thousand, for there would be four times as many who would come to hear a popular truth as to hear an unpopular truth, and you have voice enough to make them hear." I say, "Get thee behind me, Satan." I would rather lead five souls into heaven than twenty thousand into hell. The redemption of the gospel is a perfect farce if there is no ruin. "The whole need not a physician, but they that are sick." "If any one, though he be an angel from heaven, preach any other gospel than this," says the apostle, "let him be accursed." There must be the midnight ride over the ruins before Jerusalem can be built There must be the clicking of the hoofs before there can be the ring of the trowels.

Again. My subject gives me a specimen of busy and triumphant sadness. If there was any man in the world who had a right to mope and give up everything as lost, it was Nehemiah. You say, "He was a cup-bearer in the palace of Shushan, and it was a grand place." So it was. The hall of that palace was two hundred feet square, and the roof hovered over thirty-six marble pillars, each pillar sixty feet high; and the intense blue of the sky, and the deep green of the forest foliage, and the white of the driven snow, all hung trembling in the upholstery. But, my friends, you know very well that fine architecture will not put down home-sickness. Yet Nehemiah did not give up. Then when you see him going among these desolated streets, and by these dismantled towers, and by the torn-up grave of his father, you would suppose that he would have been disheartened, and that he would have dismounted from his horse and gone to his room and said: "Woe is me! My father's grave is torn up. The temple is dishonored. The walls are broken down. I have no money with which to rebuild. I wish I had never been born. I wish I were dead." Not so says Nehemiah. Although he had a griet so intense that it excited the commentary of his king, yet that penniless, expatriated Nehemiah rouses himself up to rebuild the city. He gets his permission of absence. He gets his passports. He hastens away to Jerusalem. By night on horseback he rides through the ruins. He overcomes the most ferocious opposition. He arouses the piety and patriotism of the people, and in less than two months, namely, in fifty-two days, Jerusalem was rebuilt. That's what I call busy and triumpant sadness.

My friends, the whole temptation is with you when you have trouble, to do just the opposite to the behavior of Nehemiah, and that is to give up. You say: "I have lost my child and can never smile again." You say, "I have lost my property, and I never can repair my fortunes." You say, "I have fallen into sin, and I never can start again for a new life." If Satan can make you form that resolution, and make you keep it, he has ruined you Trouble is not sent to crush you, but to arouse you, to animate you, to propel you. The blacksmith does not thrust the iron into the forge, and then blow away with the bellows, and then bring the hot iron out on the anvil and beat with stroke after stroke to ruin the iron, but to prepare it for a better use. Oh that the Lord God of Nehemiah would rouse up all broken-hearted people to rebuild. Whipped, betrayed, shipwrecked, imprisoned, Paul went right on. The Italian martyr Algerius sits in his dungeon writing a letter, and he dates it "From the delectable orchard of the Leonine prison." That is what I call triumphant sadness. I knew a mother who buried her babe on Friday and on Sabbath appeared in the house of God and said: "Give me a class; give me a Sabbath-school class. I have no child now left me, and I would like to have a class of little children. Give me real poor children. Give me a class off the back street." That, I say, is beautiful. That is triumphant sadness. At three o'clock this afternoon, in a beautiful parlor in Philadelphia—a parlor pictured and statuetted—there will be from ten to twenty destitute children of the street. It has been so every Sabbath afternoon at three o'clock for sixteen years. These destitute children receive religious instruction, concluding with cakes and sandwiches. How do I know that that has been going on for sixteen years? I know it in this way. That was the first home in Philadelphia where I was called to comfort a great sorrow. They had a splendid boy, and he had been drowned at Long Branch. The father and mother almost idolized the boy, and the sob and shriek of that father and mother as they hung over the coffin resound in my ears to-day. There seemed to be no use of praying, for when I knelt down to pray, the outcry in the room drowned out all the prayer. But the Lord comforted that sorrow. They did not forget their trouble. If you should go this snowy afternoon into Laurel Hill, you would find a monument with the word "Walter" inscribed upon it, and a wreath of fresh flowers around the name. I think there has not been an hour in sixteen years, winter or summer, when there was not a wreath of fresh flowers around Walter's name. But the Christian mother who sends those flowers there, having no child left, Sabbath afternoons mothers ten or twenty of the lost ones of the street. That is beautiful That is what I call busy and triumphant sadness. Here is a man who has lost his property. He does not go to hard drinking. He does not destroy his own life. He comes and says, "Harness me for Christian work. My money's gone. I have no treasures on earth. I want treasures in heaven. I have a voice and a heart to serve God." You say that that man has failed. He has not failed—he has triumphed. Oh, I wish I could persuade all the people who have any kind of trouble never to give up. I wish they would look at the midnight rider of the text, and that the four hoofs of that beast on which Nehemiah rode might cut to pieces all your discouragements, and hardships, and trials. Give up! Who is going to give up, when on the bosom of God he can have all his troubles hushed? Give up! Never think of giving up. Are you borne down with poverty? A little child was found holding her dead mother's hand in the darkness of a tenement-house, and some one coming in, the little girl looked up, while holding her dead mother's hand, and said: "Oh, I do wish that God had made more light for poor folks." My dear, God will be your light, God will be your shelter, God will be your home. Are you borne down with the bereavements of life? Is the house lonely now that the child is gone? Do not give up. Think of what the old sexton said when the minister asked him why he put so much care on the little graves, in the cemetery—so much more care than on the larger graves, and the old sexton said "Sir, you know that 'of such is the kingdom of heaven,' and

I think the Savior is pleased when He sees so much white clover growing around these little graves." But when the minister pressed the old sexton for a more satisfactory answer, the old sexton said: "Sir, about these larger graves, I don't know who are the Lord's saints and who are not; but you know, sir, it is clean different with the bairns." Oh, if you have had that keen, tender, indescribable sorrow that comes from the loss of a child, do not give up. The old sexton was right. It is all well with the bairns. Or, if you have sinned, if you have sinned grievously—sinned until you have been cast out by the Church, sinned until you have been cast out by society, do not give up. Perhaps there may be in this house one that could truthfully utter the lamentation of another:

"Once I was pure as the snow, but I fell—
Fell like a snowflake, from heaven to hell—
Fell, to be trampled as filth in the street—
Fell, to be scoffed at, spit on, and beat;
Praying, cursing, wishing to die.
Selling my soul to whoever would buy,
Dealing in shame for a morsel of bread,
Hating the living, and fearing the dead."

Do not give up. One like unto the Son of God comes to you to-day, saying, "Go and sin no more;" while He cries out to your assailants, "Let him that is without sin cast the first stone at her." Oh! there is no reason why any one in this house, by reason of any trouble or sin, should give up. Are you a foreigner, and in a strange land? Nehemiah was an exile. Are you penniless? Nehemiah was poor. Are you homesick? Nehemiah was homesick. Are you broken-hearted? Nehemiah was broken-hearted. But just see him in the text, riding along the sacrileged grave of his father, and by the dragon well, and through the fish gate, and by the king's pool, in and out, in and out, the moonlight falling on the broken masonry, which throws a long shadow at which the horse shies, and at the same time that moonlight kindling up the features of this man till you see not only the mark of sad reminiscence, but the courage the hope, the enthusiasm of a man who knows that Jerusalem will be rebuilded. I pick you up to-day, out of your sins and out of your sorrow, and I put you against the warm heart of Christ. "The eternal God is thy refuge, and underneath are the everlasting arms."

NEW NOVELS

IN THE OPTIMUS SERIES.

THE CARE OF A SOUL.

By Mme. JEANNE MAIRET.

12mo. Illuminated Paper Cover. Profusely Illustrated.

"The author of this novel is the daughter of the famous artist, Healey, who, after a sojourn of years in Paris, has recently returned to Chicago. . . It tells of a woman's sacrifice of self. She loves a man who, unconscious of her love for himself, loves her sister. The heroine nobly gives him up, and after his marriage to her sister he is accused of murder. To save and shield him she lays bare the innermost secrets of her heart."—*The Chicago Mail.*

"The book is one of the few French novels which can justly be said to be both pure and interesting. It has the vivid and artistic touch which is the greatest strength of the French school without the blase tone which permeates nearly all of the French novels which are flooding the American market, and the most exacting reader must admit that it is none the less strong and interesting for this lack. The illustrations are excellent—far above the usual standard of even the better paper novels."—*The Chicago Times.*

www.ingramcontent.com/pod-product-compliance
Lightning Source LLC
LaVergne TN
LVHW011202110826
845150LV00006B/1290

9781425572518